WARSAW 1944

The Stackpole Military History Series

THE AMERICAN CIVIL WAR
Cavalry Raids of the Civil War
Ghost, Thunderbolt, and Wizard
In the Lion's Mouth
Pickett's Charge
Witness to Gettysburg

WORLD WAR I
Doughboy War

WORLD WAR II
After D-Day
Airborne Combat
Armor Battles of the Waffen-SS,
    1943–45
Armoured Guardsmen
Army of the West
Arnhem 1944
Australian Commandos
The B-24 in China
Backwater War
The Battalion
The Battle of France
The Battle of Sicily
Battle of the Bulge, Vol. 1
Battle of the Bulge, Vol. 2
Beyond the Beachhead
Beyond Stalingrad
The Black Bull
Blitzkrieg Unleashed
Blossoming Silk against the Rising Sun
Bodenplatte
The Brandenburger Commandos
The Brigade
Bringing the Thunder
The Canadian Army and the Normandy
    Campaign
Coast Watching in World War II
Colossal Cracks
Condor
A Dangerous Assignment
D-Day Bombers
D-Day Deception
D-Day to Berlin
Decision in the Ukraine
Destination Normandy
Dive Bomber!
A Drop Too Many
Eager Eagles
Eagles of the Third Reich
The Early Battles of Eighth Army
Eastern Front Combat
Europe in Flames
Exit Rommel
The Face of Courage
Fatal Decisions
Fist from the Sky
Flying American Combat Aircraft of
    World War II
For Europe
Forging the Thunderbolt
For the Homeland

Fortress France
The German Defeat in the East,
    1944–45
German Order of Battle, Vol. 1
German Order of Battle, Vol. 2
German Order of Battle, Vol. 3
The Germans in Normandy
Germany's Panzer Arm in World War II
GI Ingenuity
Goodwood
The Great Ships
Grenadiers
Guns against the Reich
Hitler's Nemesis
Hold the Westwall
Infantry Aces
In the Fire of the Eastern Front
Iron Arm
Iron Knights
Japanese Army Fighter Aces
Japanese Naval Fighter Aces
JG 26 Luftwaffe Fighter Wing War Diary,
    Vol. 1
JG 26 Luftwaffe Fighter Wing War Diary,
    Vol. 2
Kampfgruppe Peiper at the Battle of
    the Bulge
The Key to the Bulge
Knight's Cross Panzers
Kursk
Luftwaffe Aces
Luftwaffe Fighter Ace
Luftwaffe Fighter-Bombers over Britain
Luftwaffe Fighters and Bombers
Massacre at Tobruk
Mechanized Juggernaut or Military
    Anachronism?
Messerschmitts over Sicily
Michael Wittmann, Vol. 1
Michael Wittmann, Vol. 2
Mission 85
Mission 376
Mountain Warriors
The Nazi Rocketeers
Night Flyer / Mosquito Pathfinder
No Holding Back
On the Canal
Operation Mercury
Packs On!
Panzer Aces
Panzer Aces II
Panzer Aces III
Panzer Commanders of the
    Western Front
Panzergrenadier Aces
Panzer Gunner
The Panzer Legions
Panzers in Normandy
Panzers in Winter
Panzer Wedge, Vol. 1
Panzer Wedge, Vol. 2
The Path to Blitzkrieg

Penalty Strike
Poland Betrayed
Red Road from Stalingrad
Red Star under the Baltic
Retreat to the Reich
Rommel's Desert Commanders
Rommel's Desert War
Rommel's Lieutenants
The Savage Sky
Ship-Busters
The Siege of Küstrin
The Siegfried Line
A Soldier in the Cockpit
Soviet Blitzkrieg
Spitfires and Yellow Tail Mustangs
Stalin's Keys to Victory
Surviving Bataan and Beyond
T-34 in Action
Tank Tactics
Tigers in the Mud
Triumphant Fox
The 12th SS, Vol. 1
The 12th SS, Vol. 2
Twilight of the Gods
Typhoon Attack
The War against Rommel's Supply Lines
War in the Aegean
War of the White Death
Warsaw 1944
Winter Storm
Wolfpack Warriors
Zhukov at the Oder

THE COLD WAR / VIETNAM
Cyclops in the Jungle
Expendable Warriors
Fighting in Vietnam
Flying American Combat Aircraft:
    The Cold War
Here There Are Tigers
Land with No Sun
MiGs over North Vietnam
Phantom Reflections
Street without Joy
Through the Valley
Two One Pony

WARS OF AFRICA AND THE MIDDLE EAST
Never-Ending Conflict
The Rhodesian War

GENERAL MILITARY HISTORY
Carriers in Combat
Cavalry from Hoof to Track
Desert Battles
Doughboy War
Guerrilla Warfare
Ranger Dawn
Sieges
The Spartan Army

WARSAW 1944

An Insurgent's Journal of the Uprising

Zbigniew Czajkowski
Translated by Marek Czajkowski

STACKPOLE
BOOKS

Published in paperback in the U.S. in 2013 by

STACKPOLE BOOKS
5067 Ritter Road
Mechanicsburg, PA 17055
www.stackpolebooks.com

Cover design by Wendy A. Reynolds

Printed in the United States of America

10 9 8 7 6 5 4 3 2 1

Library of Congress Cataloging-in-Publication Data

Czajkowski-Debczynski, Zbigniew, 1926–1999.
  [Dziennik powstanca. English]
  Warsaw 1944 : an insurgent's journal of the uprising / Zbigniew George Czajkowski ; translation by Marek Czajkowski.
    pages cm. — (Stackpole Military History Series)
  Originally published in Polish as: Dziennik powstanca (Kraksw : Wydawn. Literackie, 1969).
  Includes index.
  ISBN 978-0-8117-1315-3
  1. Czajkowski-Debczynski, Zbigniew, 1926–1999. 2. Warsaw (Poland)—History—Uprising, 1944—Personal narratives. I. Czajkowski, Marek, translator. II. Title.
  D765.2.W3C9313 2013
  940.53438'41—dc23
                            2013025159

Contents

List of Plates

Soldiers marching out of Warsaw after capitulation.

In liberated Warsaw.

The author after liberation in 1945.

The author in 1999 looking at a commemorative stone engraved with names of fallen colleagues from his squad.

Introduction

After the defeat in 1939 Poland was occupied by Nazi Germany and her Eastern territories by the Soviet Union. A Polish Underground was formed which comprised of clandestine educational systems, social organisations, the Boy Scout movement, and a military resistance movement. Many young people considered their duty to join. Military battalions were organised from Boy Scout units. In 1941 the German-Soviet war began and by 1944 the Soviet army had advanced into Poland. The military command of the Home Army (the *Armia Krajowa* or AK) decided against an uprising in Warsaw at that stage and most weapons amassed in the city were despatched in the Spring to the partisans outside Warsaw. However, when the Soviet army approached the River Vistula in July 1944, the command decided to liberate Warsaw by itself. The Uprising began on 1 August. Because of the shortage of arms and ammunition, particularly those suitable for fighting in built-up areas, practically no German strong-points were taken and no East-West road or strategically important train routes were intercepted. After the first week of fighting the insurgents lost their offensive initiative and for almost two months thereafter defended themselves in isolated districts which the Germans took over one by one, up to the beginning of October 1944, when the City Centre surrendered. The heaviest battles took place in the city districts of Wola and the Old Town. Most of the highly trained Scout units in these districts suffered heavy losses, and almost all the survivors were wiped out in the district of Powiśle, when they tried to join the Polish battalion under Soviet command that took part in an unsuccessful crossing to the western bank of the Vistula.

The author of *Warsaw 1944 – An Insurgent's Journal of the Uprising* belonged to the generation of independent Poland which became known as the 'Columbus Generation'. These were admirable young people, in most cases teenagers in 1939. Born into a free and independent Poland after the First World War, they were trapped in the events of the Second World War. They experienced its cruelty and if they survived, in many cases left Poland to become emigrés in many different countries around the world.

Zbigniew Dębczyński was born in Warsaw to a family of doctors. His father, an army surgeon, died in a car accident when Zbigniew was very young. His mother was a well known and much respected doctor, devoting herself to many, mostly poor, patients. During the German occupation she became deeply involved in the Underground Resistance movement, working closely with the High Command of the Home Army. Her activities were discovered by the Gestapo who broke into their apartment and shot her on the spot. Zbigniew who was in the next room, managed to jump out of a window, slide down the drainpipe into the courtyard and escape.

From that moment life for this teenage boy was one of conspiracy, using the name of Czajkowski from then on. He continued his education in a secret study group organised by the teachers of one of the top Warsaw schools, the Lelewel. Teachers would go from one private house to another, at the risk of dire punishment, teaching small groups of pupils. At the same time he was involved with Underground Boy Scout movement, which took the name of 'Grey Ranks', with aims different from those of the pre-war years (although perhaps not that different from those set by the creator of the movement, Baden-Powell).

In 1942, at the age of sixteen, Zbigniew already belonged to the so-called Battle Schools (BS) concerned, among other things, with minor sabotage. He then joined the Assault Groups (GS). Apart from intensive training he took part in a number of subversive acts against the occupying forces. That period of his life and his activities are briefly described in his journal.

In August 1943 a new Scout Battalion was created from those who took part in military action. It was named 'Zoška' after the pseudonym of the recently killed commander Tadeusz Zawadzki. When a sister battalion was formed in 1944 named 'Parasol' ('umbrella') Zbigniew was transferred to it as a patrol leader. His commanding officer was the battalion's second-in-command, the poet Krzysztof

Kamil Baczyński, later recognised as one of the greatest poets of his generation.

At the start of the Uprising, the 'Parasol' went into action in the district of Wola. But orders did not arrive in time to Zbigniew's patrol. It found itself instead in the Theatre Square and fought there in the first days of the Uprising. On the fourth day of fighting his superior officer Baczyński was killed. The description of his death in Zbigniew's journal, which appeared in the Polish Press in 1948, was a valuable account of the early days of the Uprising and the circumstances surrounding the death of the great poet.

Warsaw 1944 – An Insurgent's Journal of the Uprising is an exceptional book, written in plain, unpretentious prose, and its reader is moved by its authenticity, directness and restraint. It is instinctively a work of great literary merit. Concise, almost dispassionate descriptions of many terrible experiences in the short – and at the same time long – month of August 1944 in the Old Town, the main period on which the author has concentrated, make a strong impact. Here Corporal 'Deivir' (his pseudonym) not yet eighteen, commanding a patrol of colleagues of a similar age, after years of preparation in conditions of conspiracy, set out to defend his and their city from the hated and cruel occupiers. He was deeply conscious of his responsibility for them. Already twice wounded he tried to protect them as much as he could, yet the situation continued to develop in the worst possible way. In the final days Corporal 'Deivir' became a helpless witness while they, one by one, almost to the last one, perished. Superhuman efforts to help the wounded were thwarted by renewed, ever worsening blows. No reader will forget such scenes as the attack on the Stawki Street, the burial under rubble of the hospital in 'Pamfil', or the last fight by the Town Hall. In these hundred pages of 'Deivir's' account is contained the whole magnitude of heroism and futility in battle.

The book belongs to the documentary literature genre, factual and truthful. There is a total absence of pathos and what one might call hero-making, either of the author or the events. There is no drawing of morals or looking for the guilty parties in the tragedy either. The facts he describes speak for themselves. (He had subsequently expressed his opinion in articles written by both of us and published in the emigré press, that the decision to launch the Uprising should be regarded as a mistake.) His rational account in the journal is set in a deep emotional context on the human level. He emphasises in his introduction that from the perspective of years later he found himself 'in the happy situation' where he 'could study in peace and work in a field totally different and distant from the events which are the subject of this book'. He dedicates it to 'friends and colleagues who had less luck, but first and foremost to those for whom those years did not exist'.

The third part of the journal describes concisely the second month of the Uprising. After repeated but abortive attempts to cross from the City Centre to the district of Czerniaków, where the remains of the Parasol battalion defended themselves until practically total annihilation, the author fought on the barricades near the Polytechnic. He was commended for the Cross of Merit, which he never subsequently claimed.

After capitulation he was taken to a PoW camp, Stalag XP in Sandbostel near Bremen in Germany. After liberation he went back to school. He matriculated from a Polish school set up in Lubeck. Although I too was in a PoW camp in Sandbostel, I only met Zbigniew in Lubeck. He was to become my closest friend for a great many years. Together we came to England where Zbigniew finished his engineering studies at the Polish University College (affiliated to the University of London, with teaching in English).

He was a brilliant engineer. At first he worked for several British firms before starting his own company and enjoyed many professional successes.

We often discussed and carried within us the Warsaw Uprising in which we had both taken part. We were critical of the way it was planned and executed. Both of us published in the emigré press reviews of books on this great and tragic topic which appeared in Poland after the political ban was lifted as result of the 'thaw' of October 1956. Zbigniew also maintained contact with those associated with Parasol living in Poland. In 1999 we took part in the unveiling of a plaque in memory of K.K. Baczyński and in a commemorative ceremony which took the form of a grand spectacle on the Theatre Square in Warsaw. Zbigniew talked about the places where they had fought and where Baczyński had died. I read out my poem dedicated to the poet. This was to be Zbigniews's last visit to

Poland. He died in October 1999 in London. His ashes rest in the Powązki Military Cemetery in Warsaw, not far from his colleagues.

This remarkable man is gone. What remains are memories of him and his extraordinary, deeply moving journal.

Bolesław Taborski

Author's Note

After many years, when I wandered around the streets of Warsaw I had last seen from cellars, barricades and piles of rubble, that world seemed as unreal as if it had been on the moon. Only the manhole leading to the sewers on Długa Street was the same and greeted me as one of its old friends warmly with its round entrance. I hope it will never have to accommodate any more seventeen-year-olds.

It is a moment of reflection considering I am writing this fifty-five years after I had gone down that hole. Yes, for me studies, work, family and retirement became real. I had not become yet another inscription on the stone monument in the Parasol sector of the Powązki Military Cemetery in Warsaw: 'Deivir' [my pseudonym] 3 Comp., age 17, Aug. 1944, Old Town.

This book is for the most part a journal I had kept for a few months after the Uprising and finished shortly after the war. It was not written with publication in mind, merely the impressions of a seventeen-year-old insurgent jotted down without a specific aim, hence entirely candid. I had not planned to share them with anyone. After the twenty-fifth anniversary of the Uprising I had changed my mind and the first edition was printed in 1969. Half a century later, preparing for the second edition, I decided not to change or add anything to the period from 26 July to 2 September. I have added a chapter on the days before the Uprising – a small insight into the lives of a group of youngsters from that time, and another on the final days from 3 September to 8 October.

At the start of the Uprising there were ten of us in our squad. Three survived the Uprising and are still alive at the time of writing.

To those seven comrades and friends for whom the years that followed did not exist, I dedicate this book:

'Gryf' (Roman Wojtowski), age seventeen
'Zorian' (Zbigniew Romaniszyn), age eighteen

'Kruk' (Wacław Przypkowski), age seventeen
'Lis' (Bogdan Dworakowski), age sixteen
'Walgierz' (Napoleon Wolski), age eighteen
'Bohun' (Ireneusz Jędrzejewski), age seventeen
'Butrym' (name unknown), age seventeen

The names stated are their pseudonyms. It was unwise to know the names and surnames of comrades in the Conspiracy so as not to give them away under torture, if caught.

Zbigniew George Czajkowski
February 1999

Acknowledgements

I wish to thank The Polish Underground Movement Study Trust for permitting me to reproduce, without charge, most of the photographs. I am indebted to the late John Brown for reading the original typescript and his comments and suggestions.

PART ONE

Days before the Uprising

May 1943 – The Briefing

Actually, that's a bit of an exaggeration. We are sitting around chatting, waiting for the instructor to arrive and give us the next weapons-drill. Last time it was about the Parabellum (German standard issue, 9mm side arm, an excellent weapon). The instructor was probably somewhat surprised when at the end of the lesson all the boys in my squad could swiftly both take it apart and re-assemble, blindfolded without making a single mistake. Of course nobody owned up that they had done it before. This is our 'conspiracy within the Conspiracy [of the Resistance movement]'. We have a secret pistol in our squad, property of 'Gryf'. We are sure that if the powers that be knew about it they would take it away for those older and more important than us. We are only, after all, boy scouts in the *Szare Szeregi* (lit. Grey Ranks) of the BS.[1] For the time being we are only given instructions, fighting with weapons comes later, when we finally progress to the legendary GS.[2]

This morning we had an 'exercise' which I thought went well. In fact, I must say I was quite pleased with myself. It went like this.

For a long time, even before I joined the Resistance, I had been involved with the 'Minor Sabotage'. Its purpose was to lift the spirits of Poles and dampen those of the Germans, many of whom were in Warsaw on their way to the Eastern Front. To start with it involved painting graffiti and sticking up posters, but later it became a fairly big exercise, sometimes even partly coordinated through London. All over Europe, people were painting a big V (*Deutschland Verloren*, or Germany Defeated) or a swastika hanging from a gallows. We've spent lots of time playing this game as well.

Shortly after I became squad leader, we found out what had happened to one of the other squads in our area. Two lads were calmly daubing a wall, protected by a third on the other side of the road whose job it was to look out for any approaching patrol or some other danger. Everything was going well, when an ordinary looking

[1] BS – *Bojowa Szkoła* (Battle School), as our instructors from the underground movement (probably trained by SOE in England) called it, was made up of groups of boy scouts preparing to fight with arms.
[2] GS – *Grupy Szturmowe* (Assault Groups), later battalions named Kedyw. During the Uprising it included, among others, the battalions Parasol and Zośka.

man, walking past the painters, suddenly pulled out a weapon and marched them off to the police station, from where they were taken to Szucha.[3] The lad on the other side could only stand back and watch as there was nothing he could do to help.

I decided I could not lose anyone just for painting stupid graffiti, as no one ever came back from Szucha, so I came up with a plan, which I was actively promoting, although it was not making me very popular.

'You probably think you're some general planning the Verdun offensive,' remarked my friend 'Zorian'.

The plan was very simple, but it needed to be coordinated carefully. This morning, we assembled in the Mokotowska Street. We arranged it for as early as possible, immediately after the lifting of the curfew. Of course, no one acknowledged anyone else, we pretend we were there by accident.

So, at the end of Zbawiciel Square is 'Hanka', our liaison, holding a rolled up newspaper under her arm. Quite simply, if she takes it in her right hand, the danger is from the right, and if in the left, then from the left. At the next crossing is 'Lis' who can see round the corner into Koszykowa Street. The signals are the same. In this way we can 'see' what's going on around us. On the other side of the street from where the action is to take place is the protection – 'Gryf' with the Parabellum, and I with a hand grenade, to cover our retreat, or if we come up against a motorised patrol.

At last, the action begins.

'Zorian' paints, while 'Walgierz' is keeping visual contact with the rest of us. This way, 'Zorian' does not have to keep a lookout and can concentrate on his painting, which is going swimmingly. We move at lightning speed. The whole group, guided by my hand signals, moves from one block to the next. We've nearly covered the whole of Mokotowska Street when 'Zorian' gives me a sign that the paint is running out. I give the signal to end the exercise. 'Zorian' starts putting the nearly empty paint can into a paper bag he's brought along for this purpose. 'Hurry, hurry.' I'm sending telepathic signals across the street as 'Gryf' mutters from behind me.

[3] The headquarters of the Gestapo were located on the Aleje Szucha (the Szuch Avenue) in Warsaw. It was a given that nobody taken there left alive.

'Look out! From the right.'

'Zorian' drops his paintbrush and bends down to pick it up carefully. No one wants to be caught with fresh red paint on them. We have to make our way back through the streets rapidly filling up with people.

Suddenly, I see danger out of the corner of my eye. Through a gate, only a few metres from us, comes a figure in a navy blue or black uniform. Huge bloke, probably not a policeman, maybe some German support organisation. What's he doing here at this time? This is not a German district. Seeing some tart, probably. No time for further reflection, because he's running over the road towards our boys, shouting in some language that could well be German. At the same time he's pulling at the flap of his holster on his belt, but it's slipped around his back. Fortunately, he's not doing a good job, because the flap is secured, and he's carrying a leather briefcase in his other hand. He doesn't notice 'Gryf' or me. It's all over in seconds. 'Gryf' and I run after him and reach him just as he grabs 'Walgierz' by the collar of his coat. 'Walgierz' is small and slight, this bloke is huge. I don't know how it's all going to end, but 'Gryf' arrives just in time with a drawn pistol.

'*Hande Hoche!*' he shouts. The bloke now realises there are four of us. He throws his briefcase aside and starts running. That gives us an excellent opportunity to get his weapon, so we chase after him. 'Gryf' is ahead, I'm running behind. 'Gryf' tries to shoot, but has left the safety catch on. He stops for a second, and the bloke disappears around the corner with surprising speed.

'Leave it!' I call after 'Gryf'.

The final score:

1. Street painted successfully
2. Nobody got killed
3. We failed to get another weapon
4. In the briefcase we found some female underwear and a ham roll.

June 1943

Every few steps, pedestrians on Marszałkowska Street are greeted with an unpleasant sight. A sizeable shop is draped with a huge

German banner. In two front windows were arranged 'holy objects', namely portraits of the Führer full face and in profile, and at the back, copies of the 'bible', *Mein Kampf*, and other such rubbish.

'Today is going to be a special day for you!' I say to myself with some satisfaction, cycling past. The pockets of my jacket are weighing me down, not because of a weapon or a grenade, but with several huge steel bolts, wrapped in brown paper.

On the corner of Złota and Zielona streets, I meet 'Gryf' and 'Lis'. Both are on bicycles.

'Got the paint bombs?' I ask Lis.

'I've got six!'

Our paint bombs are old light bulbs with the tops taken off and filled with paint – yellow, green or metallic red.

We ride down Marszałkowska Street. On the corners of the crossroads on either side of our objective, stand our 'semaphores'. They are holding their briefcases in their right hands, a signal there are no patrols lurking around the corner. We ride up to the bookshop. They have replaced the huge front windows since our last visit. Despite the early hour there are already quite a few passers-by. We've timed our approach to coincide with a tram coming in the opposite direction. 'Lis' and I dismount, 'Gryf' holds our bicycles. When the tram comes past with a loud screech, I give the sign. We start the bombardment without waiting to see the outcome. Our purpose was to smash both windows so that we could hurl the paint bombs inside the shop, but they've replaced the windows with some cheap glass! The bolts pass through them as if through paper, leaving only small holes. The tram has long passed, and the window display remains as before, hardly touched. I tell 'Lis' to throw the paint bombs at the shop sign, and huge yellow and red flowers burst into bloom on it. I'm thinking that's just about the end of the exercise, when 'Gryf' comes up with a smart idea. Huge pieces of broken asphalt lie nearby, left over from some road works. He grabs a hefty chunk and hurls it at the display. The glass shatters, and Mr Hitler takes a pasting. I do the same on the other side. By now it's high time to leave, we are getting frantic danger signals from the corner of Świętokrzyska Street. We get on our bikes and disappear around the corner sharpish.

July 1943

Today, we are going to the cinema.

Just like those 'pricks who go to the flicks',[4] says 'Zorian' as we pass an old slogan painted on the side of the building, incompletely cleaned off. We are not going to the cinema as part of the Minor Sabotage, not for entertainment either, as all the tearful, sniffling, sighing 'dumplings' (girlfriends of German officers) have left for the time being. We are not even under orders.

We are going just for a laugh.

We head for the first-class cinema on Złota Street, known to the Germans as *'Helgoland'* and is *'nur fur Deutsche'* – exclusively for the Germans. Our entertainment, though, will be different to that of the Nazi 'aristocracy', hurrying to the premiere of the latest film. Our amusement will come not from the screen, but rather from the audience itself.

The preparation for this unique operation was long and arduous. For a few days the boys in the squad have been busy ... brushing fleas off dogs. We are carrying the bounty in two small bottles. About 450 in total. Through the glass we can see them bustling around in a tight crowd. There are all sorts, some small, some large, some frankly huge, but all extremely unimpressed by their long fast. As self defence against these vengeful beasts, we've loaded our socks and around our collars with at least half a box of flea powder.

We enter the cinema. 'Zorian', who speaks fluent German, buys the tickets. The huge cinema is practically empty. We take our seats, 'Zorian' at the front, I in the middle. After a while, we decide that the seats are not to our liking.

'Shall we sit at the back?' shouts 'Zorian', in German.

'Jawohl,' I reply (pretty much all the German I know).

We move to the back row, needless to say, without our little friends.

The show begins, not only for the Germans, but also for us. From the back row we have an excellent view of the progress of our insect army. It turns out brilliantly. Starting with the intense scratching

---

[4] *Tylko świnie siedzą w kinie* (lit. 'Only pigs go to the cinema') – a popular rhyming graftiti outside cinemas reserved for the Germans and the *Volksdeutsche*, German sympathisers and collaborators.

of some bastard *Volksdeutsche* and moving on to an elegant officer, everybody near the 'strike zones' is shifting uncomfortably in their seat and looking suspiciously at his neighbours. A few suddenly get up and leave. I see 'Zorian' is trying not to laugh with some difficulty. Then I feel a sharp stab in my sock. I have some sympathy for the flea. So many days without food! I give 'Zorian' a nudge.

'Perhaps we should get out of here.'

August 1943

It's six-thirty in the morning, time of the normal morning rush at the Grójecka train station. In amongst the crowd of traders and holiday-makers, I catch a glimpse of some of the lads in ones and twos, each carrying a small parcel containing their breakfast. Pretending we do not know each other, we take our seats on a train travelling out into the country, to Góra Kalwarii. It's a beautiful day, and the little steam engine huffs and puffs, pulling a dozen or more carriages with some difficulty.

We disembark separately at two stations, half at Zieleńc, half at Chojnowa. Each pair vanishes quickly into the woods growing alongside the track. After a good hour we reach the assembly point. The area has already been secured by 'Gryf's section, who arrived ahead on bicycles. 'Zorian' orders everyone to fall in and takes the report. A welcoming *'Czuwaj!'*[5] echoes around the forest.

We begin. To start with, an hour of not-so-popular drill. Not too bad, we're making progress. We take a short break, during which I inspect the pickets. I must complement 'Gryf', they are excellent. We have mapped out and memorised a network of ditches and paths which link together, and can protect ourselves over a wide area. After the break we divide ourselves into two groups. One group digs foxholes at the edge of a clearing in the forest, the other tries to capture them. Our faces are streaked with dirt and sweat by the time I order a midday break. According to old scouting custom, we light a small fire. I throw some potatoes onto the coals.

Once we finished eating, the mood improves, and soon the songs begin. *'Hej, chłopcy, bagnet na broń!'* ('Hey, boys, fix your bayonets!') rings so loudly through the trees, I have to tell them to keep it down.

[5] *'Czuwaj'* (lit. 'Be prepared'), the standard greeting and farewell of the scouting movement.

May 1944

A few minutes after four, I arrive at 'Zorian's place. We're going to meet 'Kruk's section in Hoża Street where 'Zorian' will teach them some weapons drill. Today, 'Kruk's boys will see a bolt action rifle close up for the first time.

'Zorian' is not at home, he is due back any minute, but I can see the rifle is here, as the barrel is sticking out from under his duvet. After a while 'Zorian' arrives, holding a rake he has borrowed from the neighbours. We quickly wrap the rifle in brown paper, take the rake and an old handle from a spade, and fasten them firmly together with string. Then we roll up the whole package in newspaper so that it resembles a bundle of garden tools.

I load a round into the breach of the Parabellum, check the safety catch, and tuck it into the waistband of my trousers. We're ready. Let's go!

We leave by the back door. At the gate, an old lady wants to chat. 'You boys off to the allotment, then?'

One of 'Kruk's boys is waiting on the corner of Zielna and Złota streets. He's going to lead us. All this was painstakingly organised beforehand. A lot depends on the smallest details.

We get to the corner of Widok Street, and I see the guide, who is already on Sikorski Avenue, suddenly tuck the briefcase he's carrying under his left arm – 'danger from the left!' We halt at the crossing. The guide turns back and walks past us back to Widok Street. We follow at a distance. Walking up Bracka Street we see the same signal, but this time from the right. Rotten luck! I realise now what's happening. A German patrol must be going along Sikorski Avenue towards Nowy Świat. After a while the guide confidently crosses the road. The way is clear! Once I cross the road, I see the German patrol from the corner of my eye, about 50 yards away. They've stopped a young man and are checking his papers. We make it to the other side and get to our destination without further mishap.

Seated at a round table are six boys. The oldest is eighteen, the youngest sixteen. I order them to fall in. During the report I see curious eyes constantly flicking towards the bundle we left standing in the corner of the room as we entered.

'Zorian' starts the tutorial. First he goes over the theory we covered last time, and checks to see if they memorised it.

'What's the calibre of the barrel?'

'7.9mm!'

'Good. What are the principal components of the self-loading rifle?'

'Barrel, breech block, firing pin, extractor, mainspring, trigger mechanism, magazine, fore and rear sights, bayonet, sling!'

They've learnt it well. Not surprising. We're talking about weapons. Weapons that every Pole dreams about!

Their eyes light up as six pairs of hands tear away the string and paper. The gun is in perfect condition, gleaming as it certainly did not in the hands of its previous owner, a fat German who had a habit of hanging around in the wrong places. 'Zorian' takes out five practice rounds.

'What? Only wooden bullets?'

'Don't worry, the time will come to fire it for real.'

Oil glints off metal in the light of the gas lamp. Nimble fingers assemble and disassemble over and over.

'*Czuwaj!*' I call, on my way out.

They are too preoccupied to notice me leaving.

June 1944

A few days ago we got word that 'Staszek' had been executed. We already knew there had been a raid and that he had been arrested. 'Staszek' had been one of our older friends who had moved over to the GS ahead of us. He had always been very keen on cars and had been in the Moto section.

I remembered him from one of our first operations when we had at last progressed from the Battle School to the Attack Groups. It was very tense. Maybe not for the more experienced, but for us younger ones it was a big thing. The acquisition of vehicles was always in demand, especially as they were often lost, as for example, in the famous assassination of Kutschera.[6]

---

[6] *SS-Brigadenfuhrer* and *Generalmajor* of the *Polizei* Franz Kutschera, the head of Gestapo in Warsaw, and responsible for ordering approximately 300 executions per week, was killed outside his headquarters on 1 February 1944 in an operation involving twelve underground soldiers who rammed his staff car with another vehicle and shot him at point blank range. The Germans retaliated the next day by publicly executing 100 people suspected of links with the underground movement.

We went in an armed patrol along Marszałkowska Street. A girl was leading, followed by 'Staszek' and myself. On the other side of the street was the protection – 'Zorian' with the Sten gun, 'Gryf' with a *filipinka*.[7] Behind us was another lad, unarmed, but ready to warn us of any danger. The plan was simple. We would wait for a suitable vehicle to stop, ask the driver to get out of the car, and drive off with it. We had a garage ready and waiting on Czerniakowska Street to hide the car.

As in so many operations, a big build-up and then nothing happens. We walked around like this for an hour. At one point, we thought we were in luck. A rather clean-looking car pulled up and an important looking chap got out of the back, leaving his driver behind. Just as we were approaching, the driver suddenly sped off. We were not sure whether he caught the sight of us crossing the street, or if he was going anyway. We, on the other hand, found ourselves standing nearby as protection, and what did we see? 'Zorian' was wearing a long overcoat, all nicely buttoned up at the front so that no one could see the loaded Sten gun under it. The magazine of the Sten is loaded at right angles into the side of the gun, and when concealed is worn on a long sling around the neck with the magazine pointing backwards between the legs. Everything was great, except for the long magazine protruding between the tails of his coat! We'd been strolling up and down this crowded street for an hour! Who knows who had spotted him, and whom they had told. Either way, no luck that day, so we called off the operation.

But that was then, and today is Staszek's funeral. His family managed to buy back his remains, and his closest comrades are organising the burial. We've also sent a delegation: 'Zorian' and I are the protection once more. I'm not sure what our superiors would have said about it if they had known, but we are going anyway. How can you not attend a comrade's funeral?

The ceremony is taking place at the Powązki cemetery. At the grave side will be family and close friends. We arrive on bicycles and approach no one, or give the impression that we have anything

---

[7] *Filipinka* – a crude, but effective, grenade made from a large can filled with explosives and bits of scrap metal.

to do with what is going on. But given that this is occupied Warsaw full of police and the Gestapo, it is quite an occasion. There are a fair number of people, carrying flowers, saying prayers and giving speeches. We watch from a safe distance, maybe 200 yards or more. Our job is to protect from the Wola district side. In the event of the Germans finding out about the ceremony and organising a raid, we would throw grenades and then retreat through the bushes towards the wall. This should hold them back long enough to warn the others and give them a chance to escape in the other direction. One of our grenades is the notorious 'kilo-*filipinka*'. I hope we don't need to use it. It's very effective, but you have to throw it from behind a substantial cover to escape the blast, and there is none to speak of around here.

In the end nothing happened. After a while, people surrounding the grave moved away, which was the signal for us to leave. We could not resist a look at the grave. There were masses of flowers and a wreath with a red and white ribbon with 'To Staszek – from his Comrades' on it.

I don't know why, but we took a photograph.

16 July 1944
We're in the Sadyba district. It's a beautiful, warm day. Once we would have gone swimming in the Vistula. Maybe we will again some day? 'Zorian' has come round to help me with the bicycles. Now we have four, as well as my own, all 'obtained'. The best is the one we pinched from some little Hitler *Jugend* wanker on Belwederska Street. Brand new with wide tyres, so useful on the sandy paths in the woods. When are we off to join the partisans? No one knows but for the time being we are changing some of the parts around to make the bicycles less recognisable. Mud guards off mine, bell off another, saddle from a third, and so on. They are impossible to recognise, unless someone checks the serial numbers on the frames.

'Come on, let's go for a walk,' says 'Zorian', 'it's such a nice day. There are cornfields just outside Sadyba. We can take a path across.'

'There's something in the air,' I reply, 'this war must be coming to an end. The front's advancing, the Russians can't be far away. I heard the artillery last night.'

'Wouldn't it be funny if we saw a Russian tank coming our way?'

'Bloody funny, because it would have had to swim across the Vistula. And anyway, we'll probably be sent off somewhere before then.'

We walk on. Our path leads to a small wooden bridge over a stream or a ditch. There is a gypsy woman leaning against the railings. No doubt about it, the lines on her face, the clothes, definitely a gypsy. Where she came from I don't know, because the Germans took all the gypsies to the camps, or shot them on the spot a long time ago.

'Hey there, gentlemen. Let me read your palms for you.'

'She's probably come out of hiding and needs the money,' says 'Zorian'. 'Let's get our fortunes told.'

We hold out our hands, palms upwards. She scrutinises them carefully, tracing the life and death lines with her finger.

'You are going to become very seriously ill.'

'When?' asks 'Zorian'.

'Oh, not long, not long. And you are going on a long journey,' she says to me.

'Am I going far?'

'Oh, far, far away. Over the sea.'

'How long will I be gone for?'

'Oh, a long time.'

'What was she on about?' I said to 'Zorian'. 'Why on earth would you get sick? As for me, I'm not planning any long journeys.'

'Sure. In a few months the war will be over, and we'll be back in college.'[8]

17 July 1944

We're meeting at 'Zorian's place. 'Misiek', our new squad leader, is on his way. When we became an attack group our squad was reorganised. 'Misiek' became squad leader and I became second in command. Now we're more like an army. Our squad is ten people, split into two sections. We're part of a platoon, whose commander is

---

[8] A month later, 'Zorian' was dead in the rubble of the Old Town, and three months later, the author went on a long journey in a locked cattle wagon, from which he did not return.

'Mors', and second in command is 'Krzysztof'.[9] They are older than us, and have also been through officer training school, known as Agricola. They both have a badge, the letter 'A' on an oak-leaf. I am positively jealous. I'd have loved to have gone through officer training, but I'm too young and haven't finished school yet. Instead I'm on something known as the 'course for young leaders', which is where I met 'Mors', who was taking us on one of the exercises. He was telling us about the operation when they, along with 'Krzysztof', blew up a train. Meetings of the platoon leaders often take place at 'Krzysztof's' house, so I got to know him and his lovely wife Basia a lot better. I hope this location doesn't get compromised, because we seem to be over-using it.

We're getting a bit agitated because 'Misiek' is late. He's been late before, so there's no real reason for concern. After half an hour however, I tell everyone to disperse. Actually, I am concerned, because 'Misiek' told me in confidence he was going to the other side of town in the hope of buying some weapons. Maybe he'd been nabbed? I always think the worst when things don't go as planned. However, there was no alert, but even so, best be careful. 'Misiek' only knew two addresses: mine and 'Zorian's. We decide not to sleep at home tonight, so 'Zorian' will stay with his uncle on Chmielna Street and I'll stay with my aunt.

18 July 1944
I meet 'Zorian' in town. We still haven't heard from 'Misiek'. Apparently, someone who knows his address went round there, but found no one at home. I heard from someone else that there was some shooting on Grochowa Street.

We decide to play it safe and not go home tonight either.

20 July 1944
'Misiek' is dead.

As we thought, he had gone to Praga district to buy the weapons he had told me about. He was with a girl, we don't know her name, but maybe he took her along so as not to arouse suspicion, as

---

[9] Krzysztof Kamil Baczyński, already an established poet and cult hero at twenty years old.

couples invite less interest. Apparently, they escaped into a church, but the Germans broke in and shot them both. Someone saw their bodies. The details are a bit sketchy but one thing is for sure, and that is 'Misek' is no longer alive. I get a message from 'Mors'. I am now a squad leader until further orders. And we can go back home tonight, because the dead can't give out addresses.

22 July 1944
In Sadyba. Today I'm at home, which consists of a small room next to a garage in the garden. I'm hiding things that could incriminate me in the event of a raid here. I don't want to invite reprisals on the inhabitants of the house in whose garden I'm staying. I've made a hiding place in the tiled oven in my room, which has probably not been used since before the war. To get to it I remove the tiles one by one. As I replace them the cracks around need to be filled with mud from the souvenir garden, and cleaned carefully, so that it looks undisturbed. It takes a lot of work, but still ...

Now for the choice – what's 'unclean', meaning unsafe, and what's not? The inferior photographs I took and developed myself in a wash bowl? It all depends. The souvenir photos showing us on exercise: 'Gryf' is pointing his Parabellum into the distance, 'Zorian' is getting ready to throw a grenade, and I'm taking aim with a *Błyskawica* (a home-made sub-machine gun). Evidence enough for everyone to get it in the neck with no questions asked. These I must destroy because the faces are recognisable. But those others, less incriminating, where we are kneeling on the grass looking at something I can keep because you can't actually see that in fact we're examining a disassembled Mauser pistol! There are also copies of the *Warsaw Courier*, with its bold emblem of 'Fighting Poland', which we used to sell openly on the streets. That's a worthwhile souvenir – I could always say I bought them, rather than sold them.

What to do about the maps? I have a collection of pre-war 1:100,000 maps, mainly of the suburbs and districts of Warsaw. These make quite a large packet, which won't fit in the hiding place. The front is advancing and any day now we'll be off to join the partisans out in the country. I'll hide them behind a loose brick under the roof outside, for easy access.

I nearly forgot! Under the bed is a large sack full of pre-war military field-dressings. It doesn't even belong to our squad, but to the company field hospital. 'Conspiracy' at its best! What a 'clean' location! It's impossible to hide. I'll have to arrange to get rid of it.

PART TWO

The Uprising

26 July 1944 – Alert
My squad gathers together in two sections. One, at 'Zorian's place on Złota Street, the second ('Gryf's) at 'Lis's house on Chmielna Street. The orders specify we are to be in full kit. The Uprising is due to start at any moment, maybe even tonight, if rumours are true. We've heard the Russians have taken Mińsk Mazowiecki, and are advancing towards Otwock, maybe even as far as Miłosna.

'Mors' arrives, inspects 'Zorian's section, and orders them to stay put overnight. This poses some difficulties in both our locations, but what can you do? We'll have to lump it. At 'Lis's, the boys are crammed in side by side on the floor. It's not much better at 'Zorian's.

27 July 1944
The night passes without mishap. In the morning I ride off on my bicycle for the briefing. Nothing special. The mood in the city is strange. The Germans are evacuating, most of the offices are shut. Overnight we heard artillery from the front. I visit 'Gryf's section. They're in good spirits, although they are tired from spending the night on the floor. They complain about the fumes from the hooch stills. In the afternoon, 'Jana' brings orders we can move to other locations inside the city, but we're forbidden to go outside. I'm to attend daily briefings.

28 July 1944
The briefing is at 'Krzysztof's house. All the squad leaders are present. 'Mors' is half an hour late, as usual. We're discussing the sorry state of our armoury. It's supposed to supply the whole company. Why didn't they tell us sooner? Everybody is swearing and cursing. We decide to give 'Mors' a talking to.

'Mors' arrives, mumbling incoherently, saying he too was kept in the dark, but we'll manage somehow. We'll see soon enough … Tomorrow we're raiding the boot factory. From my squad only I am going. Combat briefing at 0800 in Bagno. I return slowly home. The streets are full of people standing around in front of their houses, chatting. No sign of the Germans.

29 July 1944

I cycle over to the combat briefing regarding the boot factory raid.
Present are: 'Mors' (in charge), 'Szary', 'Sławek', 'Piechocki', 'Jur', a
soldier from 'Jur's squad, and me. Our location has huge windows
on to the street, right opposite the warehouse. You can see distinctly
the whole building from our side. I'm not sure if this is wise.

We go over the whole operation in detail. We're each issued a
weapon. Then we get a message that the car won't be coming. It's
too late now to work something out, so we call it off until tomorrow,
same time. We keep our weapons. I cycle home to Sadyba.

In the afternoon, 'Zorian' cycles round to my place. There's been
an alert. The squad is gathering at the same locations. I go to say
good-bye to my aunt while 'Zorian' waits outside. She spots the
weapon under my jacket, and a moving scene along the lines of
'Johnny's off to war' unfolds. Eventually, I tear myself away, and
we ride off quickly, amidst tears and waving handkerchiefs.

When I get to the location on Złota Street, I find the first section
already there and in a buoyant mood. The second section assem-
bles. 'Zorian' reports that we'll be able to take up position in a new
location on the corner of Marszałkowska and Chmielna Streets. I'll
move 'Gryf's section over there tomorrow. 'Mors' arrives, and we go
over the start and the end of the operation tomorrow. We're going to
need several hundred field-dressing packs, which are still under my
bed at home. I can't leave my squad now, so I send 'Kruk' over on
his bike with a note for aunt asking for the key.

30 July 1944

It's raining cats and dogs this morning. I borrow a waterproof jacket
and cycle over to Bagno. The briefing is at 0730, so that we are in
position at 0800 exactly. Everybody trickles in. The whole operation
was covered thoroughly yesterday, so can be got going straight
away. We leave individually and make our way over to the factory,
through a gate and across a courtyard to the out-houses, where the
workshops are.

'Mors' goes first, followed by 'Piechocki', then me. 'Jur' stays with
his friend at the gate, keeping watch on the street. 'Szary' has
already gone to get the cart. 'Piechocki' and I wait at the entrance.
'Mors' knocks on the door. It's opened immediately. The workers

usually arrive at this time. 'Mors' enters. They try to shut the door behind him, but I put my foot in the door, and we're inside. I see 'Mors' take out his .40 pistol.

'*Hände Hoch!*'

We draw our pistols. My first objective is the telephone standing on the desk. With a sharp pull, I yank the wires out of the receiver. The others are searching everyone in the room, holding them at gunpoint against the wall. Next we move from room to room along the length of the building, gathering up everybody we meet and herding them into one small room. It's getting tight in there. 'Mors' keeps an eye on them. My next job is to keep guard at the entrance. I let in 'Piechocki' who has brought several large paper sacks for the boots. I wait by the door. Whenever there's a knock on the door, I let them in, search them at gunpoint, and push them into the room to join the others. There's over a dozen people in there now, already pretty crowded. There aren't as many boots as we'd expected, though we have a go at getting some of our prisoners to tell us if they have hidden any, but it's fruitless. A thorough search reveals none, so we pack the dozen or so pairs we found in the cupboards into the paper sacks.

Our cart arrives, with 'Szary' and two drivers. He's simply hired it just around the corner, in Grzybowski Square. The drivers must have twigged when they caught sight of the sacks being loaded, because I see 'Szary' having a quiet word with them, keeping his hand rather pointedly in the pocket of his coat. Quickly, we load up and move out. I escort the cart from behind, with 'Sławek' in front. The rest stay behind to guard the prisoners. In Grzybowski Square, 'Szary' goes into a bar with the two drivers to wait for the return of the cart, while 'Piechocki' takes the reins and we move off to Teatralny Square. 'Sławek' makes a signal to the lookout, the gate opens and we drive into the yard. The pouring rain has soaked the paper bags just as we're offloading as quickly as possible into our hiding place at the back of the shops. The bag I'm carrying splits, scattering its contents all over the pavement. Luckily, not many people notice. Quickly we pick everything up and stow it away safely. The cart moves off.

I wait for half an hour at Żelazna Brama Square to return the weapons. Nobody comes for them, so I go to meet 'Sambo' at the pre-arranged place. I take the bicycle I left at Bagno, and ride off to see the lads on Złota Street. 'Gryf's section has already taken up position at the new location – a not very large restaurant. Its front entrance is closed due to the rather tense atmosphere in the city these days. The kitchen is particularly comfortable, located in the basement under the dining room. It's well stocked, so we won't get hungry.

I head off to Hołówka for a briefing. Nothing new. We have these briefings every day in case there are any developments. On the way home I stop off to say goodbye to granny, auntie and her little daughter I met earlier on a tram. They are going to stay with auntie in Sadyba. Maybe it will be safer there.

31 July 1944

'Jana' arrives first thing with a parcel and some orders. In the parcel are various parts of German uniform, socks and such like. All new – our boys must have raided a warehouse somewhere. The orders are to make fifty petrol bombs. I send some of the boys out to look for petrol. Fortunately, we've stockpiled plenty of sulphuric acid and potassium chloride already. 'Zorian' brings bottles from the restaurant, 'Kruk' still has some metallic paint from the Minor Sabotage days, and 'Walgierz' pounds some sugar in a mortar. Before long we have a nice production line going.

The orders arrive – I'm to attend a briefing at some new location on Grzybowska Street. The number has been encoded, but incorrectly as it turns out. I head for Grzybowska Street. There's a huge crush in the street. I can spot loads of people who look even from a distance like conspirators, but fortunately there are no patrols. From time to time a Tiger tank rolls by, with a heavy machine gun on the turret, ready to fire. Sikorski Avenue is full of retreating German troops, mainly transport corps and Kalmyks. They look pretty haggard. Apparently, the Russian armoured brigade has reached Międzylesie. There are also plenty of *Volksdeutsche* fleeing with carts piled with junk. There are red placards requiring workers to dig fortifications for a city of 100,000 inhabitants.

I find the block and the house number. I knock on the door. A middle aged lady answers the door. I give the code word. She looks at me strangely, and invites me inside.

'What can I do for you, young man?'

This is a rather stupid situation and I make some excuses.

'Actually I've nothing to do with the Conspiracy,' she says pointedly, 'but if you wish to know where all the other young men carrying parcels are, then go through the courtyard, and it's the first door on the left.'

Some bloody Conspiracy! I take her advice and cross the courtyard. Sure enough, the whole group is there. 'Mors' reckons the Uprising may start as soon as tonight. We are all to be ready, and the rest of the weapons will be issued once it's begun. In the meantime, we're waiting for 4 kilos of plastic explosive, to be made into three mines. I also receive a few 500 złoty notes, to buy provisions: 1,000 złotys per day for the whole squad. Everybody is in high spirits. On the way back I buy several kilos of fruit.

I return to our location to find all the boys there, packed, ready, weapons cleaned. The plastic has arrived; it's a bit too hard. For mines it should be soft and sticky so needs to be kneaded on a work top with some Vaseline. The petrol bombs are lined up in a neat row ready to go.

We spend the whole evening sitting comfortably in the kitchen around the huge table, sipping beer, of which there's plenty, and helping ourselves to various titbits. For the night we move upstairs and push the restaurant tables together to make beds. In the silence the rumble of Russian artillery can be heard followed by an air raid. As we are at battle stations, we can only take our boots off. The boys turn from side to side talking about the coming action amongst themselves. We need to rest, so in the end I order silence.

1 August 1944

Right from the start I can feel something in the air. 'Mors' drops by to check once again if everything is in order. I'm keeping the boys in two locations. Most of them are on Chmielna street, part of 'Zorian's section is at his place on Złota Street. 'Butrym', who lives just opposite, stays at home. 'Zorian' and I go out to see what's going on and to get something to eat. There are masses of conspirators everywhere, you can spot them a mile off by their military boots and jackets, carrying parcels and hurrying to their various locations, ready for the 'concentration'.

A tank rolls slowly down Marszałkowska Street. The telephones don't work. The shops are closed. We buy some bread-rolls and fruit, paying with 500 zloty notes and getting change in kind. It's the only way now. We return to Złota Street. There's a written order: we are to gather the whole squad in one location (at 'Zorian's) as, once the Uprising starts, Marszałkowska Street may be cut off. Also, I'm to go to Foch Street at 1600 hours to pick up boots for the squad. The boys make their way over with all the kit, and it soon becomes impossibly crowded. A few need new boots, and measure up their feet.

At 1545, I take a bag for the boots, stick an automatic into my belt just in case, get on my bike and ride off. On the corner of Świętokrzyska and Marszałkowska streets I see a group of people milling around. They are all crowding around one person in the middle. I see large sheets of paper handed around. I come closer and see the familiar, but still uncut, latest editions of the *Buletyn Informacyjny*, selling at 10 złotys apiece. That's something that has not happened ever. I slow down to get one as a memento, but realise I don't have the time and ride on.

The location on Foch Street is right opposite Teatralny Square. It's a small shop selling prams. It used to be one of our hiding places. It's closed from the front, but when they let me in I see the whole group is here: 'Krzysztof', who is adjutant to the platoon commander, 'Piechocki', 'Gram', a squad leader like myself, and 'Sławek' from my squad. He is acting as our host in place of his uncle, who doesn't know – and doesn't need to know – that we are here. Only 'Mors' is missing, late as usual.

It is 1630. We are getting impatient and are thinking of dispersing, when shots ring out from the direction of Miodowa Street. Then a grenade explodes ... then another ... and a long burst from a machine gun.

'We should wait here,' says 'Sławek'.

We move away from the front of the shop. Bursts of machine-gun fire, explosions from grenades and single shots blend together. There must be a serious fire-fight going on somewhere. 'The Germans must have surrounded them in a house and they're defending themselves,' observes 'Gram'.

'Listen! Listen!' shouts someone outside. 'It must be the Uprising!'

From Napoleon Square comes the sound of more shots.

'Don't make a noise,' warns 'Krzysztof', 'we have no orders.'
'Let's just see what happens,' he adds after a while.

We sit at the back of the shop. In front of us, behind a thin pane of glass and some doors, is the street. Then, as if on a stage, strange things start to happen. At the first shots the street emptied completely, then people, mostly women, started moving about. All of them have their hands raised in the air, holding handkerchiefs. It looks very odd. None of us are now in any doubt that the Uprising has finally started.

An SS patrol in full battle dress comes running past. Then two SS men holding their rifles at the ready come past, looking warily into houses. Suddenly, a megaphone on a lamp post splutters to life: 'This is the Army Commandant of the city of Warsaw. Martial law is hereby imposed over the whole city. No one is to leave their home. Any house from which shots are fired at German soldiers will be levelled to the ground, and its occupants will be executed.'

Then the same again, in German, with the addition that all Germans and *Volksdeutsche* are to present themselves to army headquarters. This continues every half an hour until late at night. Obviously, we haven't captured the public address centre yet.

Dusk falls. The sky glows from the light of burning buildings. The sound of gunfire intensifies steadily. We hold a council of war: it's becoming obvious that we can't stay in this shop for much longer. Everybody's cursing their luck that led them to be stuck in this hole at this moment. I think about my boys, how we'd prepared for this moment for so long, and are now separated. I know 'Zorian' will do a good job, but I'd much rather we were all together. I propose that we wait until it's completely dark and then sneak out of the front door quietly, in our socks, to try and reach our positions. Unfortunately, nobody knows where those positions are, and the gunfire is coming from all sides, so we might just as easily stumble into Germans. We also have very few weapons between us, so the plan is dropped.

'Krzysztof' reckons that the best thing to do is to wait until another squad passes nearby. We could then join it and try to get back to our positions that way. 'Krzysztof' is the eldest and most senior here, so he's naturally in charge. 'Sławek' goes out through the back door to find out what's going on in the block. We've made ourselves comfortable on some old newspapers behind the counter, and wait.

'Sławek' returns, but we sense he's not alone. We guess he's with his uncle, the owner of the shop. Fortunately, it's completely dark inside, and we curl up our legs beneath us. Uncle trips over someone's trailing foot.

'It's dark in here, let me light a match.'

'Better not, uncle, they might see us from outside,' says 'Sławek' just in time.

'You're right. We have to be very careful.'

We sense that uncle is rather spineless. He checks that the door is firmly shut, and they go out. After a while, 'Sławek' returns alone. He says the atmosphere in the block is very cowed. All the tenants are huddled in the basement, shaking with fear. The announcement transmitted by the megaphones outside has done its job. There's no question any of them covering for us. 'Sławek' proposes that two of us go out with him, and he'll say we are friends of his who came round and got cut off by the start of the fighting. 'Krzysztof' picks out me and 'Gram'. Uncle looks as if he's seen a ghost. Without a word to us he starts whining.

'Ah, you're always making trouble for me! Youngsters like these, the Germans will think straight away that they're ... they're ...'

'Sławek' shrugs. 'I'm really sorry, uncle, it's not my fault. We can't chuck them out into the street now, can we? Anyway, they're good boys, no trouble at all ...'

'Well, take them upstairs and give them something to eat then,' grumbles uncle, as he dives back into the basement.

'Sławek' makes us as comfortable as possible in uncle's apartment, on the second floor. Unlike most people, I always get very hungry in tense situations. 'Sławek' takes half of a huge loaf of bread downstairs to the boys in the shop, while we admire the view from the window, which opens out towards the Vistula. There are buildings on fire everywhere I look. Rockets fly through the air. From the bridge, colourful tracer fire from anti-aircraft guns climbs into the sky. It's impossible to get a shut-eye this night. Over there is the battle we've been longing for ages, and here we are stuck doing nothing.

2 August 1944

In the morning, very early, there is gunfire in the street outside. Long bursts of heavy machine-gun fire come from the direction of the Blank Palace, replied by individual shots from the street just outside the shop. A skirmish! Our soldiers must be nearby! We pelt down the stairs into the courtyard. 'Piechocki' and 'Krzysztof' are opening the gate.

I see some of our boys running past, mostly young with red and white bands tied around their arms. They are lightly armed: pistols, rifles, some only have petrol bombs. I see an old man with a fine pair of whiskers and beard holding a naked sabre in his hand! Very 1863 (the ill-fated January Uprising against the Prussians). We ask for the officer – he's just coming, they say.

A young second lieutenant jumps across the street. 'Krzysztof' presents our section to him, and requests permission to join his squad. The lieutenant asks about our weapons, and says that they cannot spare any for us, but we can help ourselves to petrol bombs. He also hands out some arm bands, as virtually all of us left ours with our own squads. They are part of the 2nd Motor Battalion. We find out that virtually all of the Old Town, where they've just come from, is in our hands! Their section is just now attacking the Blank Palace.

We join the leading group, and run down into the cellars. As we rush past I catch a glimpse of Uncle's ashen face as he sees five chaps with arm bands and weapons suddenly appearing out of his shop as if the ground had just opened up and spewed them out.

We cross from cellar to cellar towards the building on the corner of Senatorska Street and Teatralny Place. A long time ago, the Germans ordered for passages to be made in cellar walls to allow easy entry into houses, and now it certainly has made moving around easier for us. The inhabitants of the houses, so reluctant to help before, now welcome us enthusiastically. We get to the house on the corner and regroup in the entrance gate. Some civilians arrive and start offering us things to eat. One stuffs my pocket full of biscuits, and a little old man holding a bottle and a plate of snacks demands that I have a drink with him.

'GPMG [heavy machine gun mounted on a tripod] to the third floor!' shouts the young lieutenant. 'Someone lend a hand!'

I glance at 'Krzysztof'. He nods his head and I rush up the stairs to help. On the third floor we knock down the door of the apartment. The gunner runs up to the window, sets up the GPMG and starts firing. I observe from behind the curtains as the rounds sweep the first floor opposite and just below the Blank Palace. There's nothing more for me to do there, so I run back down the stairs to join the others. A group of soldiers is running along Senatorska Street dragging a ladder, followed by another group. I run over to help. The palace has no windows on the ground floor overlooking Daniłowiczowska Street, and the first floor is silent, so we can operate undisturbed. We set the ladders under the windows, and swarm up them. A crush develops as everyone tries to get through the window together. A few moments later I get on to the ladder. The whole thing groans and sways from side to side, as everyone pushes the person ahead of him.

I climb into an expensively furbished room with plush carpets and paintings on the walls. I jump over the body of a dead SS trooper lying on the floor, and run after the others. Everything happens very quickly. We run from room to room until we reach a gleaming marble staircase. At the bottom is another SS trooper holding a rifle.

Luck is on our side: we open fire and the SS man lies on the ground with his head smashed open. The assault continues on three fronts – the first floor, the ground floor and the basement. Someone throws a grenade down the stairs. Several of us run after it to secure the cellars. Water from a punctured radiator gushes down the stairs. There's nobody in the cellars on the palace side, and there is no way through to the other side of the street.

I return to the ground floor. Heavy fire from the other side of the courtyard makes it almost impossible to move. Someone shouts to attack from the entrance gate. To do this we have to get out onto the street again. Under the arches facing Daniłowiczowska Street, I meet some boys from my group. For a few minutes we hide behind the columns as a German tank starts firing from Wierzbowa Street. I can see the rounds exploding against the front of the building. They don't do much damage, and after a while the tank moves away. Then two young men suddenly appear out of nowhere on the street. They've taken off their jackets, but their trousers, SS issue, betray their affiliation. They are taken prisoner immediately. One speaks Polish. But there's no time, as we have to move towards the entrance gate.

All of a sudden it occurs to me how strange it is to see a Polish soldier on the streets of Warsaw. It feels awkward: here I am, in broad daylight, with a red and white arm band, openly carrying a weapon. The days of Conspiracy are now a distant memory.

We have to move with our backs tightly pressed against the building to get to the only window near the gate on the ground floor. German bullets fly past less than a foot away from the wall. The man in front of me suddenly falls back, spraying me with blood from a nasty wound through his hand. One of our wounded in the courtyard is calling for help. He's been shot through the belly. The Germans can't finish him off because he's sheltering behind a wall, and we can't get to him either. I reach the window and slide inside. I'm in a room the Germans used as a guardhouse. There are a few of our boys in here already, along with a dead German and a woman, probably a maid. We look for weapons. I discover a box of grenades and take a few for myself before handing the rest out. I also find loads of packets of rounds for a French *Bertier* rifle, and shortly afterwards find the rifle itself which I pass to 'Sławek'. We move on. Everywhere is empty. We get to the place where I was before. We go down into the cellars again, and break some doors down, but find nobody there. The water from the burst radiator is now ankle deep.

We come up the stairs, just as the last German defenders are being mopped up. We take five SS men prisoner, along with Frigolin, an adjutant to Leist (SS *Obergruppenfuhrer* Leist, onetime mayor of Warsaw). I start throwing portraits of Hitler out onto the street. It is greeted with jubilation by the civilians who have gathered outside in quite a large number. Several of us go out on to a balcony overlooking the street. Someone shouts a slogan, then another. Some start singing a hymn. Quite a crowd has gathered now. People are laughing and crying, but also celebrating as best they can.

Somebody suggests erecting a barricade across Senatorska Street, and everybody enthusiastically gets stuck in. In a matter of hours, a sizeable structure is constructed from paving slabs, furniture and carts. There's even an entire newsstand in it, complete with cigarettes.

I take a walk around the palace. There are plush carpets, ornate mirrors and expensive furniture everywhere. The Germans didn't steal much from here. There are huge stores of the most amazing delicacies, the best German conserves and Polish jams, and even American chocolate. Our soldiers search everywhere for weapons. A few civilians have got in and are looting what they can. Fortunately, an officer appears and throws them out. I look through some papers scattered on a desk. Among them are master copies of the Red Lists, of names of people to be executed, which had so recently struck terror into the inhabitants of Warsaw. I take a few for a souvenir.

Our group receives the order to take up position in the City Hall. We fall in and move out. We've got more weapons now and hand grenades. We report to the major who is the officer commanding the City Hall. He cannot give us any news of our own squad, but for the time being orders us to join up with the section based in the City Hall. It's around midday by the time we set up position at the rear of the building on the first floor, looking out over the prison. The prison is in our hands already and the battle for the Bank of Poland is continuing. They warn us not to go into a certain room as there's an unexploded device in there. I take a look all the same. On the table is a stick-grenade, with the cap removed but the detonator cord still attached. I make it safe, and stow it away in the knapsack I acquired in the fire station along the way. 'Piechocki' found a beautiful gleaming helmet there, which he is now covering in paint, and sprinkling with sand. It looks most ... original.

Suddenly, gunfire from the front, from Teatralny Square. A runner appears.

'Hurry, hurry! Everybody to the front!'

'What's up?'

'The Germans are attacking! They might already be in the City Hall.'

We start running. In the first courtyard we hear shots close by. Two soldiers are running from the entrance gate. We see an officer with a pistol in his hand rush out and bar their way.

'Stop! Where are you going?'

'The Germans have broken in! They're everywhere!'

We rush towards them. Without warning, 'Gram' punches one of the retreating soldiers right in the jaw. I grab the other one's rifle. He releases it without a struggle. I notice at the same time he has a distinctly unfriendly face. We run into the front halls of the City Hall. It's hard to see through the smoke and dust. Bullets come crashing through the windows and ricochet off the walls behind us. In one window a barricade made out of index files is on fire. No one there, but I hear someone struggling with a jammed rifle next door. I run up to the window. On the square below German helmets are clearly visible. They are mostly hiding in the burnt out ruins of the opera house. I throw a grenade as far as I can, but unfortunately can't see the result. I crouch down in the window frame and open fire. This almost-new rifle works brilliantly. To start with my aim is a bit haphazard but settles down quickly. I am forced to keep shifting my positions as the return fire keeps hitting the barricaded windows and the frames. Someone passes me a few more loaded magazines, but I lose my target, and cease firing. The gunfire dies down. The square is empty. It's all over in a matter of minutes. We move back to our original positions. I decide to keep this rifle.

Dusk falls. We take turns keeping watch at the first floor window. The barricade stretching across Daniłowiczowska Street and Hipoteczna Street is below us. In front the Bank of Poland has fallen silent. Around midnight, during my watch, I see a squad moving in from the direction of the Old Town. They are moving in Indian file, and appear to be well armed. In the darkness we can see the white jackets on the machine pistols.

'They're our boys!' shouts 'Krzysztof'.

When we were in the 'Monkey Woods' (a centre for parachute training) our company used to paint the cooling jackets of the Sten guns white. 'Krzysztof' sends me downstairs just as the squad enters the City Hall. I don't recognise anyone. The machine pistols turn out to be only the ordinary *Błyskawicas* (sub-machine guns) with their aluminium cooling jackets. Our hope they were our boys dashed ...

3 August 1944

All five of us have been ordered to form an observation post in the tower on top of the City Hall. It's a fantastic vantage point. You can see the whole of Warsaw from the platform above the clock. Those who dare can climb a few steps up a spiral staircase to the highest balcony. On a day like this you can see the surrounding countryside for several kilometres in all directions. Occasionally, bullets punch through the metal plates covering the tower with a loud bang and ricochet around the steel framework. The Germans can see anyone climbing the spiral staircase through the little window, and try to hit them by firing blindly into the tower. Equipped with a pair of binoculars and comfortably hidden at the very top I examine our situation carefully.

I look out towards the forest on the far bank of the Vistula. The Russians are supposed to be there, but there is no sign of life, nothing to indicate that a front is advancing. In the Praga district I see a few burning houses, the largest near the Kierbedzia bridge. Huge balls of black smoke climb into the sky. The Schicht Palace on the near bank next to the bridge is on fire. Many houses in the centre of the city have Polish flags flying from them. Warsaw is currently in our hands. To the west I can see right along a wide road, the Elektoralna Street. It's completely deserted, divided by eight barricades within a few hundred metres of each other.

Around midday we witness a savage battle. Two German tanks appear from around the corner and start firing from their main cannons, trying to clear the barricades from the street. I can see every detail through the binoculars, even the shells fragmenting as they hit the fronts of houses. The barricades disintegrate in a shower of shattered stones and beams. The report of the cannons is inaudible over the general sound of gunfire to which we have already become accustomed as an everyday occurrence. I can see the tanks struggling up the barricades and climbing over them. They make it over the first and the second. The nearest is nearly over the third and is making its way towards the fourth, when suddenly objects fall onto the tanks from the windows of the tenement houses lining the street. Some of them carry a small spark with them. All explode on the tanks in long sheets of flame. Impossible to see who threw them. To us, watching a kilometre away, this battle between the tanks and the seemingly empty tenements makes a chilling impression. Instantly the whole street fills with smoke and we can't see any more.

Beyond the rubble of the ruined Opera House the Germans are still moving into Piłsudski Square both on foot and in armoured cars. We send a runner to ask for permission to have a go at them. Then a tank starts firing onto the roof of a very tall building on Napoleon Square. We reckon the Germans are getting annoyed by the Polish flag fluttering from its summit. The shells don't have much of an effect on the reinforced concrete edifice of the building, only some planks come away from the wooden superstructure and fall slowly from the sixteenth floor to the ground. After the sixth or seventh shot the flag disappears. Seeing what's coming next, 'Krzysztof' orders us to take down our flag. 'Gram' and I only hung it on the very top of the tower that morning. It's very long and looks fantastic. It took quite an effort to lug the long flagpole up the spiral staircase. Hurriedly, we take it down, half expecting the Germans to grab the opportunity to try and pick us out with a machine gun.

Sure enough, just as we are coming down from the top balcony, a long burst of machine-gun fire rakes the tower from top to bottom. We throw ourselves headlong down the stairs. The Germans concentrate their fire just in front of me. Bullets shatter the banister, sending splinters up into my face. One more leap in full view across the window and we take cover unscathed behind the stone wall. We get permission to shoot at any German we see.

I'm not too sure of my aim to start with, so I hand over my rifle to a better marksman than me. Every few minutes we fire a short burst. At first the Germans, unaware they are under fire, go about their business as usual. I observe what's going on from one side. One of the Germans crossing Piłsudski Square suddenly sways and falls. Unfortunately he gets up again and runs for cover. It is difficult to hit a moving target at that distance, but one of us manages it. Others pick up the fallen Nazi and drag him away. My go now. A group of officers and soldiers emerge from the Brühl Palace. It's a fantastic stroke of luck. I shoot as best I can, but somehow can't see any results. They start running and jump into a car parked in the square. Now I've got you! I load another clip and fire one shot after the other. Every one bang on target, I'm sure of that! Another clip. The car starts to move but comes to a halt. I fire again. Finally it gets moving. Another five shots and it disappears around the corner into

Królewska Street. I'd love to see the fruits of my labour, but never mind.

The section commander comes to visit our observation post and advises us to keep a strict lookout. The situation is not too clear at the moment, so every detail could provide useful information. I take up position by a window facing north from where the whole of the Old Town and the district of Żolibórz can be seen. I thought this section of the town was in our hands but a long burst of fire from a heavy machine gun sent directly to my position quickly proves me wrong. They must be firing from far away, because they miss the window by at least a metre, covering me with fragments of plaster. I'll have to be more careful.

We are just tucking into recently acquired, very delicious tins of meat when there is a sudden cry.

'Tanks!'

Sure enough. We can hear the screech of tracks from the direction of the Krakowskie Przedmieście. We wait nervously to see if they are coming in our direction. Six tanks are moving along Nowy Zjazd ... and ... cross the bridge instead. We breathe a sigh of relief. A runner is sent with the message that the danger has passed. Then, quite unexpectedly, we see more tanks, very close this time. Two Tiger tanks enter Piłsudski Square and head straight towards us.

'"Deivir", leg it to the command post with a message.'

'On my way.'

I stand up from my position and rush towards the stairs. At that moment, just as I am running almost upright past a large window something rushes past my nose. There is a loud report and I fall down the stairs. First impression – I've banged my right elbow against something solid. Then my hand starts to hurt. They've hit me. Uncertainly, I move my fingers. It's not too bad, except that blood starts trickling down my sleeve and drips down onto the stairs. This tower was never that high before! At the bottom I run into 'Sławek' on his way back.

'Go to the command post and tell them there are two Tiger tanks heading across Piłsudski Square. I'm a little hurt and can't go myself.'

'What's up?'

'Nothing, nothing; just a scratch!'

'Sławek' heads off, while I go looking for a dressing station. They greet me with enthusiasm; I'm only their second casualty. The nurses help me out of my jacket and wash my elbow. Blood is oozing from a small hole. The doctor arrives.

'Mmmm, we'll have to sort this out. I can see a fragment of the bone.'

He starts rummaging in his tool bag.

I start to squirm.

'Maybe ... Maybe you can fix it without cutting me open.'

'Well, maybe, but I must warn you that it will take a long time to heal. Five weeks at least, but with an operation it might be only three. Surely you want to get back to the action as quick as you can?'

Yes, I am in a hurry to get back to the action, but I also have a deep-rooted suspicion of the butchering profession. So they bandage me up beautifully and I lie down on the bed to rest awhile.

Suddenly, there's a flash and an incredibly loud bang. Somewhere very close. Then another bang followed by the clatter of rubble falling on to the metal roof. The windows of the room I am in look out over the courtyard behind the tower. There's another report, then another. They must be firing at the tower. I shudder to think what may be happening to my friends who are still up there. I rush up to the window. Above me the tower is completely shrouded in thick smoke. The falling rubble forces me back. I think of my friends I've left behind. Such good friends! It's an abysmal loss.

The doors of the dressing station suddenly fly open and a monster crashes into the room – completely covered in dust and bits of rubble. He is holding a rifle that looks as if it has been dug up from somewhere. Three similar individuals follow him. I recognise my friends. The nurses leap to their feet looking eagerly for any wounded.

'No need! We've just come to visit our pal,' says 'Piechocki' taking his helmet off. I'm incredibly relieved.

'How did you get away?' I ask, as they sit down and start to look more human.

'Gram' tells the story: 'Ah well, the first shot went straight under us. We threw ourselves down the stairs. At that moment a second shot hit and collapsed the whole framework around us. 'Piechocki' nearly bought it. Look!'

Sure enough his entire battle dress is sprinkled with tiny bits of shrapnel.

'Then it turned out the first shot knocked out the stairs below us, so we had to jump 15 feet straight down. We were half way down when our old position was completely blown away.'

'That was lucky!'

'You could say that!'

We sit around chatting for another hour after which my friends went off to take up new positions in the Blank Palace.

4 August 1944

The pain in my arm kept me awake the whole night. It's eased now and I feel a whole lot better. It's been hectic these last few days so I'm catching up with my rest. It feels very strange lying here doing nothing while the front line is right next to us and a constant gunfire from the barricades can be heard. I brood over my rotten luck. What a mess! To take a hit so early on. Five weeks the doctor said! By that time the war will probably be long over.

Actually, it's quite pleasant here. Apart from me there's only one other wounded. An elderly fellow, the one shot through the hand during the assault on the palace. He's hardly ever here though, always ferreting around and bringing back old bits of furniture. What the hell for? And so, I'm the sole focus of attention of nine pretty young nurses and an elderly lady who is in charge of them. After lengthy negotiations I'm allowed to get up and walk around as long as I don't leave the dressing station. See? There's nothing wrong with me after all. The section commander dropped in. He was very cordial. My friends also came by. They say I might be awarded something. What for? I think they're just taking the piss.

The burial of the five Germans taken prisoner in the Blank Palace is taking place in the courtyard just under the windows. A few minutes ago they were executed for belonging to the SS. As I am looking out of the window somebody speaking in German offers me a wristwatch. What do I need it for? Instead my neighbour takes it gratefully. Also not far from here is Mr Frigolin, adjutant to Mayor Leist. He's lying in a closed room and can't move his legs. It seems he managed to fall from a first storey window during his arrest and put his back out a bit. He's held pending trial by our commanders. One can look at him through the keyhole should anyone want to.

They send me over to the Maltański Hospital on Bankowy Square for an X-ray and a dressing. It's my first trip into town. I pass through the gates of the City Hall impatiently, to see how it looks. Hipoteczna Street is still behind the front line and is completely empty. When I turn into Długa Street, I cannot believe my eyes. The street is full of people, mainly civilians, but also soldiers with armbands. Lots of happy faces, all the houses are decorated with red and white flags, signs stuck on every other doorway: 'Command post', 'Chief of Staff', etc. National colours and portraits of our leaders are hanging everywhere. It all looks very festive.

I ask for directions to the hospital – through the cellar, across the courtyard, over the plank covering an enormous crater, through the hole in the wall and I'm there. There are lots of wounded there. I'm told they are from the much heavier fighting going on around the Wola District.

I look around to see if there is anyone I know here, but no. Sister in charge shows me to the X-ray department. I catch a glimpse of the screen while being X-rayed. The bones of my arm and a narrow channel running straight through my elbow are clear to see. They tell me to present myself to the operating theatre. I leave the room, pause for thought in the corridor ... then, a quick turn to the left, a hole in the wall ... and I've disappeared! After all, I could see for myself there's nothing wrong with me.

I retrace my steps back to the City Hall. As I arrive at our position, I'm told the stretcher-bearers have been sent out to pick up some wounded from the Blank Palace. I tag along with them. In a room in the corner of the palace with a beautiful thick red carpet, nurses are lifting a body onto a stretcher. Most of his head has been blown away and he is unrecognisable.

Back in our positions, I catch up with my friends who, with rifles at the ready, stand by the windows waiting for the Germans as they appear from time to time around the ruined Opera House. Apparently, 'Krzysztof' has taken out a few Germans with a hunting rifle he found in the palace. I can't see him anywhere though.

Just as I'm crossing a courtyard there is a loud drone of engines above me. Several squadrons of twin engined Junkers high up in the blue sky fly towards the east. The windows shake from immense explosions coming from the direction of Żelazna Brama Square. I hear the whistle of bombs falling closer by. As I dive into a gateway, a strange roaring sound comes from the direction of the courtyard. I look up cautiously. Something is burning brightly with a light blue flame. This we remember from 1939. The aeroplanes move on. The sky is clear apart from several pillars of smoke rising from where the bombs fell. I walk past the prison down to Daniłowiczowska Street. A two-storey block of flats is engulfed in flames; people are frantically trying to save their belongings from the burning interior. Somebody nudges me painfully. Nothing here for me to do, so I go back.

That evening there's the funeral of one of our fallen from the Blank Palace. A hole has been dug in the courtyard and several people are gathered around it. The body is laid out, covered in paper. Just as the body is lowered into the grave I notice a small oak leaf (a badge of the Conspiracy Officer Cadet Corps) sewn onto the sleeve of the battle dress. I look closer at the body. I hadn't paid much attention earlier. It's 'Krzysztof'! They hadn't told me earlier on purpose. His grave is quickly filled in. The congregation sings a hymn; the captain says a few words. The ceremony's over. Only at this moment I realise that we've lost a close friend.

'Gram', 'Piechocki' and 'Sławek' decide to try and find the rest of our group. Apparently there are some assault groups out in Wola. Unfortunately, I can't go with them, so we go our separate ways.

5 August 1944

Nothing to do after breakfast, so I spend the morning mooching around the dressing station which occupies a couple of rooms on the ground floor of one of the offices in the City Hall. It's completely quiet. I give the elderly sister a hand laying out instruments in glass-fronted cupboards. It's all looking very clean and tidy.

I hear aeroplanes in the distance. Somebody starts shouting outside, 'Air raid, air raid!' We stay where we are, sister to finish laying out her instruments and I to avoid painful knocks in the dark cellar just below us. The sound of engines comes closer. The aeroplanes are just above our heads.

'They're flying low,' I remark.

Suddenly, the drone of the engines changes to a high pitch scream as the aircraft dive. The scream becomes louder, the whistle of falling bombs is right above us. Something crashes into the opposite side of the courtyard. A moment of silence – then a terrifying explosion. The windows fall down, followed immediately by more whistles before explosions shake the building again. Instinctively, I huddle close to the wall. We look at the ceiling as cracks appear. It sags as if about to fall in, but only a huge chunk of plaster falls to the floor.

The explosions die away and a thick cloud of smoke and dust covers everything. It's so dark I can't see my hand in front of my face. The ensuing silence is interrupted only by what sounds like a siren wailing in the distance. After a few minutes the dust settles. Sister looks reproachfully at her scattered instruments. I go out to see the damage. What used to be the entrance to the Blank Palace is now a gigantic pile of rubble, as is the whole palace, in fact. A limousine standing in the entrance has been squashed completely flat, but the horn has got stuck and blares constantly. Apparently, no one in the palace was hurt, as they all rushed into the shelters the moment the aircraft appeared. In fact the shelters had been reinforced with wooden beams by the Germans some time before, and withheld the bombardment easily. I see a few of our boys taking up positions in the rubble amongst the shattered beams and fragments of walls.

I decide to go into town to try and get news about my section. As a matter of fact, I'm not allowed to leave the dressing station, but manage quite easily through the window. Fortunately, it's quite low, so my arm does not hinder me.

The streets appear safe and busy as before, but there are many more barricades. I walk to Żelazna Brama Square, which was most recently bombarded. The streets are full of rubble so it's difficult for me to get around. Along the way I ask for any news of my section. None of the soldiers I meet can give me any information. Around Twarda Street the roads are untouched and I get to Złota Street without mishap. Just in front of the house where I left my squad, there is now a huge crater. The house itself has also been severely damaged. I ask the caretaker if he knows what happened to my boys. He tells me how surprised he was seeing an entire squad fully armed and in battledress spilling out from the house, but since then he has heard no more about them. Next I call on 'Zorian's mother. She can't tell me any more other than shortly after the start of the uprising 'Mors' arrived and took them all away. She has heard nothing more since, either. I reassure her the best I can and carry on with my search.

Somebody tells me there is an assault group stationed in Twarda Street. I make my way there and indeed there is a section calling itself an assault group. The sentry lets me in. Unfamiliar faces everywhere. Disappointed, I return to the City Hall.

6 August 1944

Undeterred, I decide to carry on looking for my squad. They tell me our section is probably in Wola. There must be something in this because if 'Gram' and 'Piechocki' hadn't found our section, they would have returned. It's a long uncomfortable journey. I had my dressing changed today and have a new sling, so my arm doesn't get in the way too much. In fact, it works to my advantage, because every time someone spots my empty sleeve hanging down, they stop to help me.

I move out early in the morning. At the moment, the main battles are being fought in Wola. The Old Town is a sort of rear echelon. People are walking around in the streets. There are lots of soldiers who have returned to the quarters here, to rest after several days of fighting in Wola. No one is carrying any weapons, as they are left behind for relieving those on the front line.

I go along Przeskok Street, which has no barricades along it. An unbelievably dirty individual in full battle dress walks towards me, a red and white arm band over a German uniform, *Błyskawica* submachine gun slung across the chest, two grenades tucked into the belt, and a pair of binoculars hanging around his neck. Quite a dashing figure I'm thinking, as he approaches.

''Deivir'!'

''Mors'!'

Sure enough, I now recognise my platoon commander. He greets me heartily.

'Cheers, chum. I thought you'd bought it.'

'Not me! But you, you sod, you jolly well deserve it.'

'Why, what did I do?'

'You should know. What kind of state was your platoon in at the start of the action without a commander or squad leaders?'

'Ah, that was a mistake. The messenger carrying the orders to me got held up by some unpleasantness. Later I went on my own, but we missed each other along the way.'

'I know the rest, but tell me how are my boys?'

'Ahh, that's a long story. They've knocked out a tank but it's better that they tell you themselves.'

'Yeah? Where are they?'

'At the moment they're resting. I'm just on my way there.'

We head back to the Old Town. I have a question going over and over in my mind, which I am scared to ask. In the end it comes out.

''Mors', have we lost anyone?'

'Oh, we've lost many.'

I look at him sharply.

''Tadek's gone, 'Maryla' too. 'Luty' is wounded.'

'Yes, but from our lot?'

'Ah yes, 'Butrym' got wounded on the second day and was taken to hospital.'

'What happened?'

'A bullet went through his lung, but he'll be alright.'

We turn off Długa Street onto Podwale and nearly collide with a tall soldier wearing a helmet. I recognise 'Zorian'. We give each other a big hug. It's not far now. A sentry ushers us through a gate on which somebody has drawn an umbrella in chalk. 'Zorian' sees me looking at it with surprise.

'It's the new emblem of the battalion.'

We go through a large and well-tended garden to what used to be a cinema, from where many voices can be heard. This is our new platoon quarters. Inside I see soldiers sprawled out over the seats. 'Zorian' leads me to a corner where already from afar I recognise my boys. Our meeting is very cordial but not carried out according to 'regulations' (a spontaneous greeting which usually involves being thrown into the air) because of my arm. Sitting comfortably amongst old friends, everything looks much brighter.

To start with everybody's talking over one another about the first days of the Uprising. Eventually I piece together what the squad got up to in my absence. They told me to start with they stayed where they were, as they had no orders after the action had started. Then 'Jana' arrived under heavy German fire, carrying orders. Under 'Zorian's command, the squad left the building and engaged fire with the Germans in the Astoria Hotel whilst waiting for 'Mors', who then led them into action in Wola.

The situation in Wola, from what I can gather, is hell on earth. Different squadrons all mixed together, fire from all sides from rocket launchers and tanks. All the petrol bombs we made together have been used on these tanks. There's no end to the stories and they carry on late into the night, but, in the end, tiredness takes over as they had only just returned from the action, and we go to sleep.

7 August 1944

We wake up very late today. The boys, because they were tired after six days of battle, and I, because I can now stop worrying about them. 'Zorian' and I go into town to look around liberated Warsaw and also to visit the wounded.

Krasiński Square looks like a carnival. The sun is shining and there are crowds of people wandering about. Somebody has even set up carousels and swings. In the distance you can hear the echoes of gunfire. Smoke from the burning Wola district is swept across the sky by the wind. From time to time a car with red and white markings arrives from the front for provisions, or an ambulance with the wounded. In the hospital of St John the Baptist there is a huge crush. They keep bringing more wounded and the hospital is overflowing. We make our way slowly through the vast wards looking for any of our friends. The wounded lie on the floor, side by side. It is very stuffy and the air is thick with the cries of the injured soldiers. Many are in a very bad way. The worst are the burnt ones: no amount of bandages can cover their huge, weeping, rotting, injuries.

In the corner of one of the wards we hear a quiet whisper.

'Hi, boys.'

It's 'Butrym'. He's lying in the corner, squeezed between two other wounded soldiers. He looks very pale but is fully conscious. He can only speak in a soft whisper. He feels fine and says he's on the road to recovery. We sit with him for about an hour. When it's time for us to go we promise to make sure somebody from the squad drops in whenever they have a chance.

We find 'Halszka' in a tiny hospital next to Nowy Rynek. A few days ago during a firefight some moron shot her by mistake with a Thompson machine gun. The bullet went through her leg just above the ankle but fortunately not too deep and she is hopeful of a quick recovery. 'Sławek', who is her fiancé, comes to visit her often, so she's heard all the latest news.

After we get back I go and see 'Lot', our former company commander, with a request for something to do.

'Mmm. Can't you carry on as a squad leader then?'

'But I'm wounded.'

'Then go home, do whatever you like.'

'Surely I can be of some use? Please. My arm is almost back to normal.'

'Well, you can become guard commander then.'

And so I've become guard commander. I've been assigned a dozen or so volunteers, all of them brand new. When possible, I'm supposed to take them through some exercises and arms drill. I post a few sentries and with the rest go through a few exercises in the square. Next come a whole platoon of novices to whom I'm supposed to teach basic drill. What the hell is the point of this right now, I think to myself as I chase these poor unfortunates, now nearly forty of them, up and down the square. A small German gun boat comes to their rescue. It's been steaming up and down the Vistula for a while now, amusing itself by shooting at any tall buildings along the banks. One round hits the church steeple next door, and the other hits the protruding edifice of the tenement near by. Small shards of stone come showering down. I shout for them to take cover and we retreat strategically behind a wall.

My friends manage to get hold of a new battledress for me, as well as a helmet and webbing. 'Kruk' helps me dress, so I don't look like some down-and-out beggar in front of the new boys. I remove my sling, put my arm through the sleeve of the jacket and support it through the strap of my binoculars. My arm feels a lot better, although I can still only move my fingers.

In the evening, I'm standing with a sentry at the front gate, when someone looking like part-civilian, part ex-policeman thrust something into my hand before walking away quickly. To our surprise we discovered it was a brand new revolver in a holster! The boys are very pleased because we're very short of weapons.

Later in the evening there's a sudden burst of activity. They're ordering everyone with weapons to fall in ready to move out. Apparently the situation in Wola is getting very serious. 'Zorian' gathers our squad and shortly afterwards, standing in the gate, I wave goodbye to a long line of soldiers as they march past. They are going to relieve the position in Wola. My squad is leading from the front and looking pretty sharp in matching battle dress and helmets. I'd do anything to go with them, but too bad ...

8 August 1944
In the morning I am relieved, no longer on duty. There's nothing to do so I kick my heels around the empty quarters. There are still a fair number of people here: volunteers, lightly wounded and the usual shirkers. I don't know anyone here apart from 'Kamil', an old friend from school, who joined our squad shortly after the start of the Uprising. Yesterday they were looking for someone who could speak German fluently and he volunteered. He spent the whole morning putting together a German uniform, and now is off somewhere, all very hush-hush. I wonder where they're sending him.

I head off for the centre of town. I'm supposed to visit the families of all my friends and reassure them, and also to find out what's going on. The once familiar entrance to Żelazna Brama Square looks completely different today. I can hear gunfire from the barricade in the distance. Half way down the street a guard stops me from going further. He advises me to go down a side street through some cellars and courtyards. I turn into a road that's been badly damaged. Not a soul in sight. I stop to check my bearings and carry on over the rubble. Just as I'm climbing over a barricade there is a sudden report, and a bullet flies just past my head. A machine gun is firing from the ruins a few metres to my right. I fall to the ground knocking my arm painfully and wait to see what happens. From the gate of a half demolished house to one side I see two of our soldiers. One, holding a MP40, is hiding behind a wall, the other beckons towards me. I scrabble over to them.

'What are you doing here?'

'I'm trying to get to the town centre.'

'What, this way? We're in a very forward position. The Germans are about to attack.'

As if by confirmation, a German hand grenade falls a few metres from us and explodes with a relatively feeble explosion. The soldier holding the MP40 fires off a couple of short bursts. At this moment, I become aware of constant gunfire coming from all directions.

'I'd love to stay with you, but I'm wounded.'

'You'd better leg it then. Go along this wall, you're least exposed that way.'

I start feeling like an unwelcome guest, and return to quarters. Only on the way back to the quarters I realise that we've been cut off from the town centre. Hmm ... not good.

In the evening, there's a Mass for the soldiers, in St Jack's church nearby. The church is full of soldiers, and quite a lot of semi-invalids like me. Civilians pack the aisles. The atmosphere is unusually upbeat. This is the first time in five years so many Polish soldiers are visible in one place. During *Boże Coś Polskę* the civilians roar their heads off and the soldiers join in. (The hymn, roughly translated: In front of Your altars, we beg you, Lord, help free our Motherland.)

9 August 1944

I'm still a bloody guard commander and it doesn't look as if anyone's coming to relieve me. The lightly wounded come pouring in from early morning. Some come on their own two feet, others are helped in by friends. All of them look pretty miserable. Their uniforms are torn and dirty, they sway on their legs from sheer fatigue. They tell us the fighting in the cemetery has been unusually heavy. During the night, the scout battalion Zośka counter-attacked with heavy losses and not much in the way of results. I think of my boys who were also supposed to be there.

'Gryf' arrives. His left hand has been torn apart by a grenade fragment. Fortunately the wound, although large, is not deep; he is hoping to return to the action tomorrow. He's recently got hold of a Parabellum (automatic pistol), which he's brought with him. We tried it out in the garden. I tried firing with my left hand, without much success. I've always been very strongly right handed. Next, 'Gram' and 'Lis' arrive. Our troublesome light machine gun is jammed again, they've been sent back with it to find the armourer. They tell me the bad news straight away: 'Walgierz' died last night during the attack on the cemetery. He took a bullet right in the forehead. They buried him there and then. He's the first to die from my squad. I leave them to rest a while on a garden bench before going back to their positions in Wola while I go over to the gate where the sentry is calling out to me.

While we're discussing the hiding place of a German sniper whose shots can be heard from time to time echoing down the streets, an unbelievable noise suddenly comes from behind the houses. A long, continuous scream or, to be exact, several piercing screeches, one after another. What on earth is that?

Something heavy is falling through the air. Instinctively, I fall to the ground and take cover deep inside the gateway. At that moment there's a blinding flash in the centre of the garden. The gateway crashes down and the blast throws us on the ground. We crawl behind a wall because five more come after the first one, each accompanied by an intense blast. You can feel the air compressing after each explosion. We lie there for some time, blinded by the smoke and dust, unsure if there's any more to come. Out of the darkness come cries for help. Slowly, the darkness clears, some outlines begin to appear. The first thing to notice, as I'm rushing back into the garden, is the sudden change of season. The trees, which a minute ago were covered in leaves, are now standing completely naked as if in midwinter. The two storey office block on the right is lying in a heap of rubble. I trip over what looks like a pile of minced meat. I can tell from the boot sticking out it was once a human being.

Someone is being carried by on a stretcher. With a shock I notice it's 'Gryf'. He's got a deep wound in his thigh, which is bleeding heavily. I rush up to him.

'Ah, 'Deivir', I've been hit, I'm afraid. Go, look for 'Lis'. We were sitting together on the bench.'

I run over in that direction, and find 'Lis' hidden under the branches of a fallen tree. He's semi-conscious, but quickly comes to. He's not wounded but completely deafened by the nearby explosion. I help him to his feet, and together we survey the scene. All the buildings around us are damaged to some degree. Half the roof of the hall where we were sleeping has fallen in. Unbelievably, none of us was killed apart from two civilians under the rubble and that unrecognisable person on the path. There's a few more, but only lightly wounded.

That afternoon we move to new quarters inside the Krasiński Palace. Over the entrance of the palace hangs a large opened black umbrella. There's a field kitchen steaming in the garden under the trees, and some soldiers lying on the grass around it. In the bushes nearby, a pair of artillery men is repairing a recently acquired 75mm anti-tank gun. A couple more from the motorised section are riding round the garden on a tractor fitted with caterpillar tracks which came with the cannon. I go for a spin with them.

10 August 1944

More bad news from the district of Wola. The Germans are attacking constantly. They back up their thrusts with concentrated mortar fire. Their tanks advance steadily, despite several losses. I can hear the battle coming closer. There's a burst of machine-gun fire. Grenade explosions and the reports of tank guns all blend into one continuing noise. Huge columns of smoke rise from behind the ruins of the Jewish ghetto. It's as if everything there is permanently on fire. In the garden and inside the Krasiński Palace, people are getting increasingly agitated. Those who are not in the action for one reason or another, pace up and down impatiently waiting for orders and keep commenting on the news. There's a constant stream of heavy and slightly wounded from the front line. Our dressing station is already full, but the main hospitals are fuller still. I wonder if there's any possibility of me getting involved in the action. Since they last changed my dressing I notice that the wound has closed over. I can now move my arm, although can't straighten it fully, but every time I knock it, it hurts like hell. I got rid of my old helmet and now have a brand new one with a fabric cover. One of the nurses sewed a badge with an umbrella on it on my left sleeve. We are all wearing these now.

Having nothing else to do, I decide to go and visit my boys. I move quickly with a column of stretcher bearers through the ghetto. It's a vast expanse covered only in piles of rubble. It looks very menacing. From time to time, a shell flies over and then all of us quickly fall to the ground waiting for the explosion. Once we crossed the ghetto I get completely lost in the confusion of the front line. There is firing ahead. Burnt out German tanks lie amongst the rubble. I make my way underneath a burning house, and completely lose my bearings. The Germans must be attacking not far away: I can hear shouted commands and bursts of machine-gun fire.

I join on to a retreating group of soldiers, and find my way back to the entrance to the ghetto. Nearby, one of our tanks is shooting somewhere into the distance. It's the last one left, and immobilised, either from lack of petrol or a damaged engine.

After a long search, I eventually find my boys inside the ghetto and crawl carefully up to their position. A few of them lie in a shallow fox hole, scraped out of the rubble. 'Sławek' and 'Lis' are here, along with some lads from another squad. The others, not far away, are fast asleep on some blanket scraps, which does not surprise me as they've been on the front line, without relief, for three days now. Our light machine gun is positioned nearby, behind a small fragment of a still standing wall. The actual front line is eighty metres away. I find 'Zorian' in a foxhole behind a pile of rubble which could tentatively be called a barricade. To the right, in a similar position, I can see 'Kruk', and 'Baszkir's helmet sticking out. I can't get to them, as it would mean I'd have to crawl very close to the ground, which is still impossible for me. 'Zorian' fills me on the situation. The Germans are about 30 metres away in similar fox-holes. Neither side can even stick its nose out, without drawing a burst of machine-gun fire, but the short distance prevents them from using mortars. Instead, the battle involves throwing hand grenades at each other. A few hours before, 'Zorian' managed to hit a German position with a Mills bomb. Apparently they heard terrible shouting coming from there. The Germans are mostly throwing their grenades blindly. At that moment, one lands about 5 metres away from us. We duck down waiting for the explosion.

'That's not too bad,' I say when it burst.

'And they don't break into many fragments either,' adds 'Zorian'. 'Ours are better from that point of view.'

I notice the huge 'gammon' (a homemade grenade, probably 1–1.5 kilograms of explosive obtained from unexploded bombs) standing in front of him, obtained from the air raids the previous night.

'I can't throw that one further than 20 metres, so I'm waiting for them to come a bit closer,' says Zorian. 'Did you know 'Kruk' threw a German grenade back before it exploded?'

That's just like him. As I retreat, I wave to him from a distance, and make my way back to the palace.

11 August 1944

Around midnight there's a sudden confusion in the quarters. Groups of civilians arrive. Everybody gathers in a hall on the first floor. I find my way there as well, to find out what's going on. We line up in two ranks. There are about sixty people here, all unarmed. They call people out in descending order of rank. Somehow it turns out that I'm the most senior here and therefore made to take charge. I get my orders to take all these people to the Tłomackie district and then await orders from a certain Mr 'Janek'.

We form a long column and make our way through the dark streets in single file, clambering over the barricades. I find Mr Janek with some difficulty. I'm told to build a barricade. Mr Janek shows me where, and disappears. I'm left alone with the group of people. The streets and the neighbourhood are completely empty. About 100 metres in front of us, buildings are on fire on both sides of the street. It's completely quiet, but for the roaring of the flames and the crack of the beams falling in.

I start handing out orders. First, I divide the group into smaller sections. One group forms a chain and pass paving stones to build the front of the barricade, the other reinforce it with furniture brought down from inside the houses nearby. Behind it we dig a trench. I'm kept busy running around. After a few hours I'm completely hoarse from shouting. It's nearly dawn by the time the barricade is ready. The barricade consists of two horse drawn carts, one car, and a pile of furniture. The pavements have been stripped for quite a distance.

Seeing as we're completely alone here, I decide to head back the way we came. I gather everyone together, and we set off. On the way, there is a sudden roar of a rocket launcher. The rockets fly just above our heads. We just about have time to fall to the ground before the first explosion, followed by several more in quick succession. All the rockets land on the roofs of the houses right on the other side of the street. There's a fair amount of dust and we're covered in small pieces of wood and tile. As we move off I count everyone carefully. No-one is missing. No-one is even injured.

In the morning I am told our detachments are retreating from Wola. Now I understand why we've been made to build barricades in positions seemingly far behind the front line. Shots fired from various calibres intensifies, and the first mortar bombs start to fall into the garden.

Around 10 o'clock there's a call for volunteers to carry dressings and ammunition to the front line. Hoping to meet up with my boys, I step forward. Three of us head off through the palace gardens. From there, we only have to cross over the Nalewki and hand over the grenades we're carrying to soldiers from the first company, who have taken up positions in one of the nearby houses. They tell me where I can find my boys. They're not far away, and when my chance companions leave, I head off to look for them.

I go along the Nalewki on the opposite side of the garden ducking down behind broken walls of houses. Suddenly there is a hiss, as something flies through the air. I fall on to the pavement just as a round from a mortar explodes a few metres in front of me. Three more land immediately afterwards. I wait for the explosions to die away and start to get up. The moment I got up a sudden burst of machine-gun fire smashes into the wall just above my head. I fall again as fragments of plaster rain down on my helmet. I hadn't expected that at all and it scared me somewhat. The fact is, I'm lying on an open street without any cover, so the situation is unpleasant. I begin to creep along the base of the wall. After 50 metres or so I find an open gate and get inside.

I find myself in an old fire station. The back door is closed. I'm stuck here forced to await further developments. I sit down in the entrance and look out over the street. It's completely empty. A ferocious gun-fight is going on not far away. Several trails of tracer fire are coming down low along the street. There's a sudden explosion, and a round hole appears in the wall on the other side of the street. There are more explosions every few seconds. I watch as a hole after hole appears on the wall, as if someone's knocking down a toy castle made out of building blocks. This is followed by a muzzle report. I realise there is a tank behind me firing over the roof of the single storey building in which I've taken shelter.

After shooting a dozen or so holes, which despite the short range (80 metres) appear to have done little damage, the tank shifts its attention elsewhere. I hear the sound of rubble falling nearby, and the sound of hobnailed boots running down the street just outside. There's a burst of machine-gun fire very close. Suddenly a figure appears in the doorway wearing a Polish helmet. His face is completely covered in blood pouring from an open wound on his head, dripping down onto his uniform and on the Sten gun gripped in his hand. I help him sit down and remove his helmet. At that moment I recognise 'Bohun', one of the boys in my squad! I tear open the field dressing and start to bandage the wound on his head. I can see it's not serious, just a long wound along the scalp, but it's bleeding heavily.

''Bohun', where did this happen?' I ask him, once he's somewhat recovered his breath.

'Just here, nearby. I was just making my way back to our boys when a tank shell went off just next to me. Luckily my helmet took most of the fragments.'

I take a look at the helmet. It's got long gouges in it.

'What's the situation?' I ask, after a while.

'The Germans are attacking. We were just running for help.'

'Where's our squad?'

'You have to get out into the courtyard, turn left through a hole in the wall and you'll find them. But I think I'll go back to the palace. My head's spinning.'

'Wait, we'll go together. I'll help you.'

'It's alright; I'll run this last bit. You can't help me when I'm running and two of us make a larger target.'

'As you wish.'

' 'Deivir' will you take the Sten gun? I don't need it now that I'm wounded. Here are some magazines. This one sticks a bit, but the other two are OK. I've only got about forty 'pips' [i.e. rounds] left.'

I take the gun and watch 'Bohun' as he runs across the street. A burst of machine-gun fire follows him, but always a few metres behind. I see him get to safety in the garden on the other side.

I'm alone with the weapon. The Sten is sticky with blood. I sit in the corner, quickly dismantle it, clean the firing mechanism with a rag, reassemble it, load an empty magazine and move my right hand uncertainly. It's still got a dressing on it, and I can't straighten the arm out fully, but one can always try. I load a single round, and fire into an empty barrel. Everything feels absolutely fine. I attach the bag with the magazines, tighten my webbing and run out in to the street. The machine gun didn't even manage a single shot before I made it to the other side.

I find my friends easily; they've taken up position in the Mostowski Palace. They fought off the German attack, but one wing of the palace is on fire. There's a civilian fire engine hard at work behind the building but it's doubtful they'll manage to put the fire out, as the Germans are in front preventing them from moving outside. I visit each of my boys one by one. I find out 'Lis' was wounded a few hours ago, and was taken to the rear, unconscious. He was hit by a shell fragment when a tank fired into his position. This is very bad news. 'Lis' was the youngest and we were all very fond of him. Now that he, 'Walgierz', 'Butrym', and 'Gryf' have gone, there are only six of us left.

'How many days is it now?' I ask 'Zorian'.

'Only eleven days, and half of us have gone already. It's my turn next.'

'Don't croak, you're not a kruk!' ('Kruk', meaning raven, traditionally considered a gloomy bird, was the pseudonym of one of the boys who actually had a cheerful disposition.)

I take up a firing position in the window on the first floor. Below us, the street is divided down the middle by a high wall. On the other side is an empty wide expanse covered in piles of rubble. This was once the Jewish ghetto. Hidden amongst the piles of bricks are the Germans. They can occasionally be seen moving around when they change position, or when reinforcements arrive. By and large, they stay out of range of my Sten gun, and only occasionally do I see something closer. I fire carefully, conserving my ammunition. 'Zorian', hidden in the next window, is having a ball. Two days ago he acquired a self-loading rifle with a ten round magazine from a dead German. He fires time and again, and several times with favourable results.

The building is burning above our heads and to one side of us. It's getting very hot. The flames and smoke are fanned by the wind towards our direction and obscure the view. It has the advantage that the Germans can't see us here. Apart from a few shots, which hit the window frame above us, we're left in peace. The fire creeps gradually towards us. Once the doors shielding us from the flames have burned down, the blast of heat is such that we have to retreat to the next position, which is on the stairs. They're made out of stone so the fire won't reach us for a while.

I hear movement on the other side of the wall, running down the middle of the street. I see two grenades flying from 'Kruk's position and landing on the other side of the wall. I give 'Zorian' two of my grenades as his supply has long run out, and my arm makes it impossible for me to throw them. I can't see the results of the explosions but it couldn't have been pleasant for anyone hiding behind the wall.

The blaze forces us downstairs. This is the last window overlooking the wall of the ghetto from our position. There is a sandbag in the window, which makes an excellent rest for our rifles. The burning door frames, three metres away, give off so much heat that it's difficult to withstand it for long. 'Zorian' and I take it in turns to keep watch by the window, swapping over every five minutes. Whilst one of us keeps watch, the other runs out into the courtyard to cool his steel helmet with water. After a while we have to swap every three, and then every two minutes. 'Zorian' manages to bag a German running back to the rear positions, probably a messenger. I too manage to win a prize in the form of an enormous military policeman who broke cover not more than 20 metres away. At first, I didn't notice him, focusing rather further out into the distance. The German stood up, certain there couldn't be anyone left in the burning building. I took aim carefully and squeezed the trigger. After two shots the Sten jammed. The German fell, obviously wounded, and started to crawl towards shelter not more than 2 metres away from him. I struggle with the empty cartridge stuck in the firing mechanism. The German was about to get away, when just above my head came two loud shots, followed by two more. 'Zorian' had just returned and fired with his rifle resting on the top of the sandbag. The German lies motionless.

'That got him,' I say, rubbing my ear, deafened by the blast. 'It's a shame we can't go and fetch his weapon.'

Shortly afterwards, the rising heat and telltale pieces of rubble falling from the ceiling about to cave in, make us abandon our position. We rejoin the rest of the boys. I discover I've only five 'pips' left from the supply given me by 'Bohun'. Unfortunately, no-one can help me out, we're all in a similar situation. I'm about to send someone back to the palace for more ammunition, but it turns out it would be better if I go myself, as they'll give me more.

And so I head back, loaded down with bottles of wine and packets of cigarettes for our wounded. In the Mostowski Palace there was a storeroom filled with lots of good things. We've saved a number of boxes of medicines and surgical instruments among other things from the flames.

Getting back to the Krasiński Palace wasn't as simple as I thought. I emerge from the cellars onto the square bathed in sunlight, and immediately a couple of bullets whistle over my head, goodness knows where from. I barely have time to take cover in a crater left from a ruined building. I wait several minutes and then move on. I'm in the bushes right at the edge of the Nalewki, and gaze out hesitantly over the open street through a hole in the fence. This stretch is familiar, but being alone doesn't boost my confidence much. In the end, I pull myself together, and sprint across the road. I'm half way across when the sparks of the machine-gun fire scatter just in front of me. I fall into a gateway. The gate is shut. I curl up inside the porch making myself as small as possible as burst after burst of machine-gun fire hits the wall a few centimetres ahead of me. I kick at the door with all my strength. Eventually my persistence pays off and at last I hear the footsteps of the janitor approaching. Instead of opening the door immediately, the moron calls out: 'Who's there?' When he finally opens the door, I tell him exactly what I think of him, and forbid him to lock it again. I make my way through the trees and bushes in the park to the palace. I immediately go to the magazine and again come up against an unexpected hindrance.

'Do you have a requisition order?'

I'm stunned. I've just come back from the front line. I must bring more ammunition for my boys and here is this man asking me for a piece of paper. I tell him precisely where he can stick his requisition order, and add a few choice comments about people who stay safely in the rear echelons.

To my surprise, two boxes of brand new 9mm rounds promptly appear on the table. Immediately I open one and load all my magazines. In the passage, one of the runner girls grabs me by the arm and hauls me in front of a large, ornate mirror hanging on the wall. Now I can see what sort of impression I'm making which explains the prompt reaction. I'm smeared all over with black soot and blood from 'Bohun's wound.

I run down quickly to the cellar to see the wounded. 'Lis' is still unconscious. The doctor tells me that even if he pulls through he'll never be quite right. The shell fragment crushed his skull just above his forehead and nearly penetrated inside. Poor little 'Lis'!

I take the long way back to the Mostowski Palace, uneventfully this time.

12 August 1944

We spend the whole night at our posts. The flames in the palace are slowly dying out, but it's still too hot to return to our previous location. The night passes almost without mishap along our section. From time to time, a rocket is fired into the air from the German positions in the ghetto, or there's a short burst of machine-gun fire. Our machine gun doesn't reply often. We have to conserve ammunition.

At dawn we hear movements, and German voices very close by. Silhouettes appear along the wall and start climbing through the gaps. We hear hand grenades spluttering as they fly through the air. In the darkness most of them miss the windows, but hit the wall and fall to the ground below. One lands in the room next door and explodes in a shower of yellow sparks. All this happens in a matter of seconds. I lean out the window and fire long bursts towards the moving figures. I see the explosions of our grenades next to the wall and cease firing as the targets disappear. Things stay quiet until daylight.

At around 10 o'clock in the morning we are relieved, and retreat from our positions. I've only been there twenty-four hours but the boys haven't slept for forty-eight. 'Zorian' and I carry some first aid equipment we've found back to a little hospital where the Pamfil Restaurant used to be, next to the Garnizonowy church. Our wounded, 'Halszka' and 'Butrym' are there now, evacuated after the bombing of the St John the Baptist hospital. The doctor in charge was a friend of my mother's. He's very grateful for the equipment we've brought him, and invites us to pop by anytime! Under normal circumstances that would have been quite funny, but these days, who knows?

We rest for a few hours in the quarters of the Krasiński Palace. 'Mors' suggests a little outing towards the German tanks in the ghetto. 'Zorian' and I volunteer. 'Janka' comes along with us. She's seen a lot of action recently, and her newly acquired 9mm Mauser seems to make her look for more. I think about taking the PIAT (Projectile Infantry Anti-Tank weapon), but the only one we have is up front, and despite recent air drops, there's not much ammunition for it, so we make do with petrol bombs and two plastic mines.

We make our way quickly through the Krasiński Palace gardens. The end of the gardens is also the limit of our territory. After a brief pause, we jump over the road one after the other. No-one fires at us. We are now in no-man's-land. We enter a half demolished house with weapons at the ready. It's empty and completely quiet. Our boots make an unpleasant sound as they grind against the glass from broken window panes. My heart is beating fast. I expect a long burst of fire to come from behind every bit of broken wall. Carefully, we lean out into the courtyard and look over the roofs and windows. Not a soul in sight. We cross over to the other side and make our way to the first floor, up stairs covered in rubble. There we find an apartment with an open door. It's right on the corner of the building and looks out over the ruins of the ghetto. There's nothing to see on this side, but when we go to the next room the first thing we notice when we look out of the window is a German armoured car standing among the piles of rubble. It's about 50 metres away, its cannon pointed in our direction, but no-one next to it. It's too far to throw a grenade.

'Shit, if only we brought the PIAT.'

Something moves in the courtyard behind us.

''Deivir', go and see what's going on.'

I crawl into the next room and peer through a gap in the wall. An old lady is scrabbling around in the rubble. Maybe she's looking for some of her possessions, or maybe someone was buried there.

'Nothing serious,' I whisper.

From this room I can see out to the side of the building. Suddenly I spot something moving amongst the rubble. A German comes into view, running towards the armoured car cursorily hiding amongst the piles of bricks. I take aim, but don't fire. From the next room comes a long burst of fire from 'Mors's MP40. I squeeze the trigger. The German falls to the ground. Good hit! I make sure with another burst. At that moment – I've no idea what's happened – everything goes black. Instinctively I throw myself towards the entrance and fall over in the doorway. Several feet tripped over me. There's a blinding flash out of the darkness.

Deafened, I find myself in the courtyard. I recognise my friends with difficulty: they look as if they were born in Africa! I see 'Zorian' taking shelter by the wall. There's a narrow trickle of blood down his blackened face. I rush over to him and take off his helmet. It's just minor wound on his temple. 'Janka', who is carrying the first aid kit, applies a small piece of sticking plaster, and we run like hell from this unlucky place to catch up with the others.

We are stood down that night and can get some rest. I'm awakened by unusually heavy gunfire. This time, it's not coming from the frontline but from all sides. Many rounds are being fired from all different calibres. I run to a window overlooking the Krasiński Square. A few boys are already here looking at the sky. It's a dark night except for the usual red light flickering from houses burning in the distance. We can see multicoloured bursts of tracer fire from anti-aircraft positions all around us. From time to time there are also individual bursts of red. These are the larger anti-aircraft guns. They are set to explode at a certain height, scattering sparks over the sky. Beams of light from powerful lamps search the clouds.

On the square is a row of little lights in the shape of an arrow. They are electric light bulbs joined by a cable. We all strain to listen. To start with, I can only hear the constant fusillade of gunfire. After a while, we can make out the distant rumble of aircraft engines amongst the shooting. Suddenly everybody's spirits are lifted. At last someone has remembered us! Help is on the way!

I look into the distance, trying to make something out in the darkness. For a split second something flickered in the searchlight. 'There, there! Look!'

We can see the silver silhouette of an aeroplane caught in the beam of light flying a fair distance above us. We wait with baited breath. The pilot jinks, and the aeroplane vanishes into the darkness. The searchlights concentrate on that spot, but he's disappeared. We breathe a sigh of relief.

Again we hear the sound of engines coming and going in the distance, followed by a loud noise of an aircraft coming straight towards us. The search beams shine low along the roofs. We peer into their light. The aircraft comes closer and closer. Suddenly, just above the roofs of the houses on the other side of the square, a huge four-engine aeroplane comes to view. In the bright light of the search beams which continue to lead it, it's silver all over. It is flying straight at us, no higher than maybe 300 feet above the rooftops. Anti-aircraft fire pours into the aeroplane from all sides. With hearts in our mouths, we see bullets slamming into the fuselage, wings and engines. I clench my fists to avoid crying out. It feels as if all the bullets are being fired straight at me. A wide shadow flashes past, and disappears into the darkness. It's only been a couple of seconds but it feels like eternity.

With a roar of engines the aircraft flies over us. We rush over to the other side of the palace. We see the aeroplane disappearing into the darkness in the direction of the ghetto, flames blazing from one of its engines. Something white fluttered above the trees of the park. We follow the red ball of flame to the limits of visibility until it disappears from view, filled with an overwhelming pity and helpless fury. Our fourteen years old messenger 'Sambo' is in tears, he who always, without hesitation, runs through the heaviest crossfire.

We get word that some of the air drops have fallen into the ghetto. Immediately I organise a few volunteers. We scrabble around in the darkness for our helmets, tighten our webbing, grab our weapons and rush down into the garden. I lead a small patrol made up from the remnants of my squad. Five of us set off at a run across the park. We pass our last position, the one we crossed on the way to the disastrous encounter with the tank, and enter the ruins of the ghetto.

Silence and void. We could come across a German patrol any minute but the boys don't hesitate. We clamber over piles of rubble making a fair amount of noise. My heart is beating loudly. I grip my loaded machine pistol firmly with the safety catch off, and press on. Other patrols are here doing the same thing. We look in every hole and crater but find nothing. A hand grenade explodes nearby. Who knows where it came from? From behind the rubble on the right I see movement, and a few shots are fired. Our three machine pistols reply in short bursts. We take cover amongst the ruins.

'Grenades!' I order.

Everybody apart from me throws one. Silence. The Germans must have been frightened off. There is some tracer fire further away towards the Stawki, but it's high above our heads, and doesn't disturb our search. In the end we don't find anything, and head back, discouraged.

We hear voices next to a ruined bunker in the corner of the ghetto, and come across several of our soldiers crouching next to a huge steel canister. It's lying right next to the place where we entered the ghetto! We give them a hand hauling it back.

It's almost daylight before we can rest again.

13 August 1944
The day starts badly. Part of the barrage from a grenade launcher lands on our building, the rest in the gardens next to it. There are cries of 'Fire! Fire! It's burning!'

From the neighbouring hall, which must have been a ballroom once, come clouds of smoke. I suddenly remember the fire extinguishers attached to the walls downstairs in the cellars. I rush down with my squad; others join us as we go. We run through the cellars taking all the extinguishers from their stands and sprint back up the stairs, two at a time, towards the fire. There are masses of people in the burning hall running around like headless chickens. Just in front

of me I see 'Zabawa' clutching a *filipinka* weighing at least a kilo-
gram.

'Stand back!' he shouts. 'The blast will blow out the flames!'

It was said that ever since he took part in the assassination of
Kutschera, 'Zabawa' has not been quite himself. I manage to stop
him just as he's preparing to throw it, and make it safe. I bang the
cap of a fire extinguisher against the ground and direct the stream of
liquid towards the flames. Others come up behind me. Despite the
fact that the extinguishers are ancient, and half of them don't work,
the fire quickly dies down. We throw the rest of the smouldering
furniture over the balcony into the garden.

We stroll around the ancient palace feeling rather pleased with
ourselves when we are interrupted by more cries from above.

'Fire! Fire!'

We run up the stairs at the double. Some of the boys are trying to
break down the doors leading to the attic. When the door finally
gives, our hands drop at the hopeless sight in front of us. The whole
attic is completely ablaze. Rafters crash down as they burn through.
The heat forces us back. The building will surely burn to the ground
now.

They order all the soldiers left in the palace who still have
weapons to fall in. Soldiers from all different sections gather in a
huge hall on the ground floor. The third company, currently num-
bering about thirty people, is ready for action. The remainder of my
squad is part of them. There are a number of other people, too, and
along with nurses and stretcher bearers, there's about fifty of us all
together. We fall in two ranks down the middle of the hall. 'Lot'
gives us our orders.

We are to advance across the ruins of the ghetto to the Stawki, and
occupy them once more. (We abandoned the warehouses situated
along the Stawki only two days ago.) We are only a part of the
attacking force though: on the right is the Anna company and
someone else's on the left. Ammunition is brought and distributed
to everyone. There's very little of it. The situation with regard to
grenades is a bit better.

Whilst all this is going on, the German grenade launchers carry
on as usual. Without hurrying, like clockwork every dozen or so
seconds, a grenade flies through the air and lands either in front of

us, or on the roof of the burning palace. Our ranks sway with every blast, but we remain where we are until dismissed. Suddenly a grenade explodes against a window. The whole rank throws itself to the ground, leaders first. One lad in our company gets a grenade fragment in his back as he falls, and is carried away on a stretcher: 'Jeremi' disappears with the others. We are left alone. Lying on the ground we check our weapons, ammunition and grenades. Everything's ready, lets go.

It's 10 o'clock in the morning. We exit into the garden and move through the shrubbery in a long line. A group of girls carrying stretchers bring up the rear. It all looks very military, I must admit.

Quickly, we cross over Świętojerska Street and into the wide expanse of the ghetto. It's a beautiful day. We can clearly see our target: the high walls of the tram depot, the apartment blocks and warehouses of the Stawki district. Between us and the target is about 500 metres of wasteland covered only in piles of bricks: all that is left of the houses that once stood here.

We're supposed to advance under cover, but it's not easy to hide a column of people this size, all of us laden down with arms and equipment, from observers in an elevated position. We had only made 30 or 40 metres before the German machine guns opened fire. Lying in a shallow depression I can hear the whistling and rumbling of bullets flying past. The air above me is pulsating incessantly. I get the impression that if I stick my nose out, even for a moment, from under cover, it will be torn to shreds by the mass of flying metal.

''Zorian',' I say, as momentarily we lie side by side, 'just listen, this is the famous 'whistling of bullets' [a line from a military song].'

'Oh, haven't you heard it before?'

I'm ashamed to admit I haven't. Up until now, in all the combat situations I've been in, the bullets flying close by were accompanied by the sound of gunfire, and the crackle of bursts as they crashed into walls and pavements. However, the novelty of this new whistling phenomenon soon wears off.

Every now and then, we have to advance over small exposed outcrops of rubble. I see bricks suddenly disintegrating around me, and small fragments flying in all directions. The first wounded begin to fall. The nurses gather them up on stretchers and disappear to the

rear, quickly returning for more. In the next hollow lies the body of
the boy who was running just ahead of me. Above me, 'Zorian' is
firing again and again from his automatic rifle. He shouts to me to
take the ammunition from the dead boy. Smeared with his blood
I fish out several dozen rounds from his cartridge pouches and
pockets. 'Zorian' throws me two magazines, which I start loading
immediately. The target is obvious. About 200 metres in front of us
the German positions can be seen clearly. Small puffs of white
smoke mark the machine-gun nests. With my next leap forward, I
catch up with 'Sławek'. Our aeroplane machine gun is rattling off
bursts of rapid fire. Further on, 'Gąsior', from the first platoon, fires
belt after belt of bullets from his Dreiser. I'm only sorry the enemy is
still out of range of my Sten gun.

We get to a place where once there was a street. The area around it
has been cleared of rubble and train tracks run down the middle of
the street. A couple of tipper carriages used to take away the rubble
are still standing on the rails.

We take cover in the rubble lining the street. The Germans are not
far away and, on a number of occasions, I've managed to open fire
on a few helmets sticking out from their positions. We lie here for
several minutes, waiting for our neighbours to catch up with us. As
we wait, there is the sound of the German defensive mortar fire
approaching. To start with they land behind us, but now they're
getting closer and rounds are exploding among us from all sides.
The only reason we don't take heavy casualties is due to numerous
dips and hollows to take cover in. Even so, after a while, we begin to
hear the cries of wounded. Someone's dragging himself to the rear
and nurses in battle dress are pulling heavy stretchers over the
rubble. Then shouts, 'Attack! Attack! Forward!'

It occurs to me this is our only option if we're not to get wiped out
where we lie. I can see some of the boys running across the street.
Lines of tracer fire come down the street towards them. One falls to
the ground, gets up and keeps running. Another falls and lies still. I
tighten the strap of my helmet and load a new magazine in to my
Sten gun.

It's hard to decide on the right moment to leave a shelter and run
out into the open. Right! Here I go! I run into the street hunched
over my machine gun. In spite of the general din I distinguish the

series from a heavy machine gun close by on the left. Sparks fly off the pavement just in front of my feet. I make it to the other side and throw myself over the rubble. Just in front of me are flashes and smoke of our grenades. Somebody is standing on the top of a ruined house firing from his machine pistol. From the corner of my eye I see him suddenly slump forward and fall on his weapon. Two Germans run out a couple of dozen metres ahead of me. Excitedly, I fire two long bursts towards them. The Sten jams. I fall to the ground and dig out the jammed cartridge. Then I see another German lying not far away. I fire a burst, then another and see my bullets tearing holes into his uniform.

Behind me someone is screaming urgently for help. I look around. There are fewer than twenty of us here and some are lying motion-less on the ground between us. We huddle deep into the rubble waiting for reinforcements. I see stick grenades flying towards us. They land here and there exploding loudly, a wooden handle flying off for several metres sideways as they do so. Not that they're doing much damage though. One lands in my hole. Frantically I try and throw it out before realising it's only a spent handle. 'Zabawa', lying right next to me, calls over asking if I have any grenades, as he's used his already. I empty my pockets and webbing and hand over all I have, keeping only an antitank grenade for myself. 'Zabawa' hurls one after another in the direction of the Germans.

Three more boys come running across the street and call to us they are the last ones. 'Lot' orders us to jump back to the other side of the road. We go one by one. Fire from every sort of weapon imaginable is concentrated along the next 30 metres of ground in front of us. The heavy machine gun is the worst among them, firing virtually along the length of the street.

In one leap I make it to the carriages standing in the middle of the street, and hide amongst the tipper trucks. The bullets hitting the steel plates of the trucks make a terrible din. There are a few bodies lying in the road, the nearest is right next to the train, as if warning me against taking cover here.

I see 'Gram' fall as he crosses over. Somebody helps him over to the other side. In that moment I leap over, and take cover safely. Most of the surviving soldiers are in one fairly deep and wide crater. 'Piechocki', 'Kruk' and I are lying to the right a few metres above them, each of us in a shallow depression. 'Lot' calls over to us to look out to the side and see if any more are coming. The ground of the ghetto is deserted, covered only in dust and the smoke of explosions.

I reinforce my position by piling up bricks all around me. I'm protected now from grenade fragments, a very important move as they fall every few seconds, at times even several at once. Through the firing hole at the front I can see German helmets on the other side of the street. I fire towards them with the Sten placed flat on the rubble. After the first few rounds the dust stirred up from the barrel gets into my eyes and the weapon jams. The bolt has jammed solid and won't budge. Lying in the bottom of my foxhole I take the machine pistol apart and clean it, which is quite difficult under the circumstances.

I hear the whistle of falling mortar bombs and several explosions very nearby to the left. I lean out to see what's happened. The crater is filled with smoke from recent explosions. Along the front wall of the crater are about six swaying figures about to slump. These are the boys who were hiding there, firing standing almost upright, when a series of grenades exploded right behind them. One of the figures is 'Zorian'.

Instantly in one jump I rush over to where they are lying. With my heart in my mouth, I gently roll 'Zorian' onto his back. He's alive, but hit by several pieces of shrapnel all along his left side, from his leg up to his neck. Apart from him there are two others also wounded, and one dead. I try to put a dressing one him but it's hopeless under the circumstances, there are just too many wounds. The stretcher bearers have already taken one of the wounded men, the other is struggling back by himself.

At that moment, little 'Sambo' jumps down into the crater. He hands 'Lot' a piece of paper. 'Lot' unfolds it, and swears under his breath.

'The attack's been called off. Retreat, boys!'

All those who can, scrabble out of the crater and disappear through the rubble towards the rear. A stretcher comes past. I recognise 'Jacek'. He's unconscious with blood trickling from his lips.

We're left alone, and lie at the bottom of the crater in silence. 'Zorian' is moaning softly.

'Can you stand?' I ask. 'There's no-one left to help us.'

'I'll try.'

I sling his automatic rifle over my shoulder. Apart from that I have also a standard issue rifle (taken from a dead German) brought over from the other side of the street, an MP40 from the dead soldier and my own Sten gun. 'Zorian' cries out and falls to the ground. I help him back to his feet. I can see the slightest movement causes him intense pain. I take his arm over my shoulders and half dragging, half carrying him, we start out towards the rear.

We clamber over the heaps of rubble, my feet slipping on loose bricks. There is not one place where the ground is even. The sun beats down remorselessly. I don't have anything to wipe away the sweat pouring into my eyes. The straps from all those weapons cut into my neck, there is a loud ringing in my ears.

We crawl along painfully slowly, avoiding the high ground, so as not to attract fire from the machine guns. After some time, it's becoming obvious we're not going to get far at this rate. Several times we fall and to get up again takes every last ounce of my strength. I change direction and take a short cut aiming for the High Court buildings in the distance.

Already on all fours we drag ourselves over piles of bricks, some of which are up to 5 metres high. Each time we get to the top I grit my teeth, waiting for the impact of one of the bullets whistling past on either side. But nothing happens. As we get to the top of one of the piles, my legs give way from under me, and we roll down the scree to the bottom.

I don't have the strength to move any further. I am so exhausted to lie on my back is utmost pleasure, staring up at the rounds flying through the air. Every few seconds, a little spot appears in the sky, rapidly grows larger and larger, and then takes the form of a little bomb which lands somewhere nearby with a whistle. I'm woken from my reverie by 'Zorian's quiet moaning.

''Deivir',' he whispers, 'have you any water?'

Quickly I come to my senses and start fiddling with the strap of the water canister strapped to my back. I hand it to my friend. Luckily, I forgot about it earlier, and it's still full. 'Zorian' looks awful. His face and hands are blackened with blood and dust, big drops of blood ooze from a number of holes in his uniform. We finish the water in the bottle which I throw away. I readjust the slings of the rifles and machine guns. Each one is terribly heavy but I can't throw away guns.

We move on. I hold on to him with all my strength. I'm scared to fall, uncertain we'll ever find the strength to get to our feet again. We come under heavy mortar fire once again. A few metres in front of us there are flashes here and there, and small clouds of smoke appearing in amongst the rubble. 'Zorian' cries out, and says that he's been hit again. I note the sole of my left boot has been cut in half. I've also got several holes in my battle dress, but I can't feel I've been hit.

I see a figure lying at the foot of a broken wall. It's the body of a young female messenger with her head completely smashed open. Eventually, we get to the edge of Świętojerska Street. Unfortunately we're in the wrong place. The wall which surrounds the ghetto runs down the middle of the street, and the hole passing through it is several metres away to the left. I see some of our boys running across to the other side. I also see bullets from a machine-gun emplacement along Nalewki Street, tracing a line of dots along the wall. To get to the hole in the wall, we would have to go back several dozen metres to get around a huge pile of rubble. Neither of us has any strength left.

I lie there for a minute thinking what to do next. I remember I still have an anti-tank grenade. Surely it would be big enough to knock the wall over. I take the enormous grenade (nearly 2 kilos of plastic explosive) out of my knapsack and prepare the detonator.

From the bottom of the crater, 'Zorian' looks at me.

'You've got to be joking.'

I hurl it as best I can with my left hand, because my right is still no good. The wall is only about 6 metres away. I'm sure I'd have made it if I hadn't tripped during my run up. The grenade falls just in front of me, but fortunately outside the crater. There is an almighty bang but that's all. The wall remains standing.

The machine gun continues to fire. It occurs to me I can probably hit the machine gunner inside his bunker. I take 'Zorian's automatic rifle and load a magazine. I crawl to the edge of the crater and take up position. I can see the bunker clearly with gunfire pouring out of it but – probably from sheer fatigue – my aim swings wildly in circles. Nonetheless, I empty the magazine and load another. Not surprisingly it has absolutely no effect.

At that moment, a high explosive grenade lands on the road between us and the bunker. After it explodes the street is shrouded in a thick cloud of smoke. This is our chance! I help 'Zorian' to his feet, and we run out across the road. From there it's easy to get to the hole in the wall. We get through it before the machine gunner realises we've gone. He fires a prolonged burst but misses us. We fall to the ground in the garden. I see some stretcher bearers with an empty stretcher. I leave 'Zorian' with them and lie down under a bush.

'What's the matter, are you wounded?' I see the face of a stretcher-bearer leaning over me.

'No, no, I'm alright. I'll be going soon, just need a bit of rest.'

After I return to the palace, I discover the events leading up to this disastrous attack. The company that was supposed to be flanking us never came in the first place because their company commander said the enemy fire was too heavy. A messenger carrying the order to retreat was killed while looking for us in the rubble. By the time 'Sambo' found us, it was too late.

I'm desperate to find out more about our wounded, but the moment I get some of my strength back, we're ordered to take up position on the barricade near the entrance to the ghetto. There I find 'Kruk'and 'Baszkir'. They tell me that 'Gram' died in the dressing station. He was hit by shrapnel in the abdomen and died from loss of blood before they were able to put a dressing on him.

'Sławek' joins us. He was helping carrying some wounded back to the hospital. He says 'Jacek' was seriously wounded and it's unlikely he'll live. It's very sad; 'Jacek' was his best friend. 'Zorian' has fourteen pieces of shrapnel in his body but fortunately none of them penetrated very deep. I'd love to go visit the wounded. The hospital on Długa Street is not far, but we can't leave our positions. There are only four of us left from our squad now, and we reminisce sadly about the recent days of the Conspiracy. We settle down close together and talk loudly about those who died.

There is no hope of being relieved from our positions soon, so we reinforce ourselves as best we can as the German grenade launchers don't give up for a moment. Every few seconds something explodes on the damaged roof above us or to one side. Our only hope is that a grenade doesn't come through a window, which is probably unlikely as they fall almost vertically. I am now in possession of 'Zorian's automatic rifle. From the upper stories of the building I have a good view of the Germans moving around on the other side of the ghetto. I fire only occasionally changing my position frequently. We don't use our GPMG at the moment so as not to give away our positions, and also because we don't have much ammunition.

Night falls.

14 August 1944

The night passes without mishap. The silence in the ghetto is interrupted only by occasional bursts of tracer fire from German heavy machine guns, but they are not aiming at any specific targets. Every twenty seconds or so, a white flare explodes in the sky: the Germans are afraid of another attack.

The Krasiński Palace burns all night illuminating us with a red light. Two fire engines work through the night in the square, pumping water from the water reservoir. Thanks to their efforts, about one third of the palace has escaped the flames. The rest has been completely gutted right down to the cellars; only the empty walls remain standing.

Around midday we're relieved from our positions. It's about time: after forty-eight hours without rest we're desperate for sleep. Walking across the square I see a small group of soldiers in battle dress helping themselves to something. I go over and join them. It turns out they've discovered a huge cauldron from our battalion field kitchen in the still-warm ruins of the palace. The aluminium lid has melted in the heat, but under the blackened crust one can fish out something which tastes quite good. It was once a cauldron full of soup, but all that's left of it now resembles a meat loaf.

I find out from them where to find 'Zorian'. The house they point out to me on Długa Street looks like a pile of ruins. The whole front of the building has collapsed under bombardment from the air. However, I can see some people clambering over the rubble, and when I follow them I find myself in the only part of the house still standing, in large room filled with casualties lying on the ground.

I find 'Zorian' straight away. He's lying on a handful of straw squashed between two other wounded soldiers looking pretty miserable. He says the staff here is ten times too small for the number of wounded, and no-one's seen to him since he was brought here. He asks me if there is any way we can get him over to the Pamfil restaurant. I can see for myself the conditions here are truly awful, so I head back to our quarters to get some help.

I bring 'Baszkir' and 'Kruk', and between us we carry him over to the Pamfil. It's much better here. There are beds, more room, and loads of friends. Amongst others, 'Halszka' and 'Butrym' are here. Unfortunately, we can't be away from our quarters any longer to find the other wounded from our squad. We still don't know what's happened to 'Gryf', 'Lis' or 'Bohun'.

We run back to our quarters, which have now moved to the High Court. There also hangs an opened umbrella over the entrance. We're not allowed to stray far from the basement, as we might be needed on the front line at any moment. Just as I try to catch up on my sleep, there's an incident outside. A mortar bomb lands in the courtyard just next to the window. The courtyard is so narrow it resembles a well, and nobody imagined any of the bombs constantly falling on the roof or in the square could land in there. The outcome is inevitable. Three of our men and two German prisoners were wounded and two more prisoners killed. The prisoners are guarded by our military police in the neighbouring building, but occasionally they are brought over to work. There's about 140 of them, all of them Wehrmacht, as all the captured SS men have been executed.

I try to fall asleep despite the din of the gramophone and my dear colleagues who are cheering themselves up one last time before they end up in the 'garden of the stiffs', as they call it. They have a point. Looking around, I see only about a third of those I knew at the time of the Conspiracy.

15 August 1944
It's still dark when the alarm is raised. To be ready for action I need only to put on my helmet, which I keep under my head, and grab my weapon with which I sleep. We stumble through the darkness as we run, to reinforce our positions in the ruins of the Krasiński Palace. In the park ahead a great commotion can be heard. People

are running through the bushes, several single shots fired, a few grenades exploding. I strain my eyes into the narrow space in front of me, barely illuminated by the glow from the flares. Somebody calls for help from the bushes, but in Polish. German voices can also be heard. We can see shadows moving around. I can't decide whether to fire or not, because some of our people might be there. Apparently, the enemy has attacked from the left, and one of our patrols is stranded in the park. We can only wait.

After a while, everything quietens down. We stay in our positions. Just before dawn, we can hear the deep rumble of artillery in the distance. That's the Russian front. The sun rises, and with it the daily dawn chorus. The first to awaken are the mortars as they start with their usual 'pik!' from somewhere along the German lines. A few seconds later, comes the whistle of the flying rocket or rockets followed by an explosion. Their favourite spot is the square behind us. Don't they know nobody walks that way anymore? Either way they keep firing. Sometimes the rocket launchers roar into life. The noise from them is quite overwhelming. We count the individual roars followed by deafening explosions somewhere behind us. Sometimes, when they don't add up, we know there's an unexploded rocket lying somewhere in the rubble, ready to be dismantled and made into hand grenades. Fire from a heavy machine gun flies through an empty doorway to my right. The Germans must have fixed it in that position, because every few seconds a burst of fire comes through the same place. The walls behind me are slowly disintegrating, a stream of fire passes right next to me. If I stick my hand out, I would lose it in a second and what would be the point of that?

Well past midday, we're relieved from our positions. I take advantage of the lull, and, after cleaning my weapon and finding something to eat, I go to visit 'Zorian'. 'Butrym' is in the bed next to him and 'Halszka' can already walk with a stick, so we're all together. We chat for some time. I begin to get the feel of the situation the wounded here are in. They lie in this hall with only sandbags in the windows as protection against all kinds of incoming fire, listening to the noises from the front line. It's no further than 300 metres to the nearest German positions. A single line of houses on the other side of the square is all that's left standing between them. I am aware now how important it is to hold our positions, and not let the Germans get through, as all the wounded here and in the other hospitals will be slaughtered.

It looks as if the fighting will get heavier, so I leave all my papers, photos and other personal items with 'Zorian' for safekeeping. They have a better chance of surviving here in the hospital. I'd like to stay longer but must go back.

On my return I make myself comfortable in a cupboard on the first floor, which is full of law books. Shutting the door behind me it feels more secure than in an underground shelter. I can still hear the explosions, and the building sways from side to side with each blast, but here lying on top of the old documents, it's nice and cosy.

When I crawl out of my hidey-hole, fully refreshed, it's already dark. It turns out my company has already left for the front line! I curse my colleague who was supposed to wake me but obviously forgot. I rush out to follow them, only to find out by the barricade on Świętojerska Street, that the third company has already advanced into the ghetto. They advise me not to follow them on my own, as it's easy to stumble into enemy lines by mistake, or even get shot by our own side.

I go to join the command post of the 1st Company. The entire command is located in some ruins, comprising one commander, one messenger and two nurses. After sitting around in the darkness for a few hours, the need to send a patrol out into the park is announced. I volunteer straight away. Along with two others I've never met, we creep out quietly into the garden. We're supposed to cross the entire park, and get to Barokowa Street. The park is shrouded in darkness and completely quiet. We get our bearings from a large building burning brightly in Barokowa Street. We make our way slowly, being careful not to make the slightest noise. A few times we hear a movement, and stand completely still until it's passed. From time to time, the park is lit up by rockets passing over our heads. When this happens we drop to the ground and watch carefully.

We're not far from our objective when a sudden burst of fire from a Schmeisser comes toward us from a bush a few metres ahead. The soldier walking behind me throws the grenade he's holding ready in his hand, and rushes forward. We run together through the bushes, shots coming from all around us. We give as good as we get, firing long bursts towards the muzzle flashes in the darkness. A vicious firefight breaks out. A few hand grenades explode behind us. We run into a group of our soldiers, who fire a few shots in our direction before they realise who we are. We take the long way round back to Świętojerska Street.

16 August 1944

We are being sent out to take up new positions. There are four of us, but from my squad there's only 'Baszkir', because 'Sławek and 'Kruk' have been sent to the rear to fetch ammunition, and have not yet returned. The route to the forward positions is very complicated. First we have to make our way through the still smoking ruins of burnt-out houses along Świętojerska Street, then find a hole in the top of the pile before sliding down into the cellars. From there on we go from cellar to cellar until we see daylight. We find ourselves in a small single storey house, half of which is lying in ruins and the sky is visible through the holes in the roof.

I'm in charge of this little group. 'Lot' puts us in the picture and then disappears, promising he'll be sending relief by the evening. We're left alone. The park around us is empty and quiet. We can't see very much, as our visibility is limited by the bushes 30 metres away. Once there was a garden in front of the house surrounded by a fence. The remains of the wire netting are still standing, hindering the approach to the building. I'm sure I could knock out a few as they climb over the netting, I think to myself as I lay out a plan of defence.

We set about barricading the doors and windows properly. We pile rubble and bricks high up in the windows, leaving only small holes as firing stations, and a way out at the back of the house. The building was previously used by the Ministry of Health, and all the windows are covered in mosquito netting, which gives us first class protection against hand grenades.

I climb the ruined stairs to the first floor and find an excellent position from which we could drop grenades on the enemy should they try to enter the house. I leave one person with most of our grenades here. The rest of us continue to reinforce the ground floor. Instinctively, we move around with as little noise as possible and talk in whispers. This turns out to be a good thing, as we soon discover when a poorly built barricade falls over with a crash. Immediately, someone outside opens fire and bullets come crashing into the walls.

Eventually everything is ready. We make ourselves comfortable on chairs, each next to his firing position. Our weapons lie by our sides, ready to fire. For the rest of the day, however, there is nothing remarkable to report in our sector. The Germans, however, are not saving their ammunition. The mortars fire without pausing. Out of boredom, I try to count the mortar bombs. I get to 304 in the course of two hours and then give up. From time to time, there's the roar of a rocket launcher. We are directly in its line of fire, but in no danger because we're fairly close to the German lines and the rockets fire above our heads. Only once does a salvo of rockets land not far away, somewhere near the palace. Several seconds after the explosion pieces of shrapnel fly over and, amongst other things, a huge sheet of metal, about 5 metres by 5 metres lands in the garden in front of us.

Dusk falls, but the promised relief does not arrive. The food we've brought with us has been eaten, and there's nothing edible in the house. Night falls and still not a soul wants to come to visit us. Now when it's dark we have to be extra vigilant because the enemy is on three sides. We fight back the tiredness by staring obstinately into the darkness stretching before us. Something moves in the bushes. I lift my rifle but it's nothing, just an illusion. A German rocket goes up illuminating the area. Nothing to see.

Suddenly, there is a movement. I can definitely hear the bushes rustling. I grip my weapon waiting for another rocket, but the darkness remains unbroken. I hear low voices. From 'Baszkir's position completely invisible in the darkness, comes a soft click of a Sten being made ready to fire. He also senses something. Suddenly the loud report of a rifle breaks the silence. It's 'Pik', stationed on the left side of the house, who couldn't hold back any longer. There is a sudden commotion out in the park. I hear footsteps running and someone struggling with the netting a few metres in front of me. I squeeze the trigger, firing in the direction of the noise. I fire again and again. Several figures can be seen by the light of the flames coming from the muzzle of my gun. I squeeze the trigger – but no luck. I change the empty magazine and fire again. Now there are flashes in front of me. Bullets from a sub-machine gun smash into my shelter in a shower of sparks. There are shouts. I'm blinded by a sudden flash of yellow flame. It's a hand grenade, followed by a second and a third a few seconds later. Frantically, I load my empty magazines. Bullets come flying in over the palisade in the window with a crash. More shouting and movement outside. To my left, I hear 'Baszkir' cursing and struggling with his jammed Sten gun. I fire another ten shots. After the last one, the bolt remains in the open position. Silence. 'Baszkir' has fixed his Sten and looks out to the front. A few rockets go up illuminating the area. I can't see anything. A grenade explodes far away in the bushes.

'Hey! You up there on the first floor, that's enough!' I shout.

Silence. We wait uncertainly wondering if the enemy has retreated for sure. No more noises can be heard other than the fire from other sectors. I do a round to make sure no-one has been wounded. Everything is in order.

'How many grenades did you throw?' I ask the soldier upstairs. 'Three.'

'There were at least six or seven explosions. The others must have been theirs.'

'Pik' reckons he saw a German fall. He must be wounded or dead, but we'll have to wait until daylight to find out more. I too heard some cries of pain, but reckon the Germans would take their wounded back with them. We return to our chairs next to the firing positions.

17 August 1944

Silence. Darkness. The flames in the nearby building die down and we can see nothing. I fight back sleep. I am alerted by a slight sound, as if someone threw a stone into the netting covering the window above me. *Psssssssss.*

It's the familiar sound of an armed grenade. Something explodes with a shower of sparks just next to the opening at the top of my palisade. Immediately afterwards there's a second, then a third and a fourth.

Instinctively, I move away from the opening. The air is filled with noise. In the brief pauses between explosions, I can hear objects hitting the netting covering the windows overlooking Świętojerska

Street and the sounds of grenades falling on the pavement at the foot of the wall. And again: *Pssssssssssssss.*

Silence returns as quickly as it was broken. I look out into the garden. Silence and darkness. 'Baszkir' opens fire a few times, but I can't see anything to aim at. The whole affair lasted maybe fifteen seconds but more than twenty grenades had exploded. Gradually, I realise what happened. A German patrol with rags tied round their boots must have crept up to the house from the side of the ghetto, and tried to throw the grenades inside. My flesh crawls to think what would have happened were it not for the netting in the windows. I'm also surprised they're not following up their initial attack with a second one. We stand by our firing positions with weapons ready, waiting. Nothing happens.

Finally, around 10 o'clock in the morning we hear someone stumbling through the underground entrance to the house. It's a messenger carrying a bucket of food. We take it in turns to eat so that three of us are always on guard. We are worried about the state of affairs. It's getting very serious. The Germans are attacking all sectors on either side of us. One of our companies has gone to help those defending the paper factory. Now we can see why we haven't been relieved, nor have we any hope for reinforcements in the near future. After leaving us a little food for later, the messenger gets up to leave, she still has to visit other positions. If they are just as difficult to get to I don't envy her.

It's a warm sunny day. The park is mostly quiet, interrupted only from time to time by a German machine gun, and of course the bastard mortars never stop. It's very hard to stay awake. Every fifteen minutes I check the others to make sure they're not asleep. I'm not far from it myself.

We take turns to clean our weapons and resume our places by the firing holes. I find a book, the only one in this rubble, and start to read about various lice and tick typhus, but soon realise that sleep will come quicker if I continue.

In the afternoon, I decide to make a small expedition out into the bushes in front of us. It feels very strange crawling over the barricades, out into the open expanse of the garden. I crawl slowly along the wall. Nothing to see. Peace and quiet. After about 20 metres of crawling on my stomach, I see something lying in the bushes to my left, but can't tell what it is. It's becoming obvious I'm not going to get far with my bad arm, so head back.

'Baszkir' volunteers to go instead. I watch him until he disappears from view into the undergrowth. He's gone for some time while we wait nervously wondering if something had happened to him. Eventually he reappears by the barricade. As he climbs over the parapet, he knocks a few bricks to the ground, which provokes an immediate burst of fire from the German lines. Fortunately, 'Baszkir' is inside by this time.

'I respectfully report, that in the bushes not far from us, is a dead German.'

He looked for weapons but there were none nearby. In the light of last night's entertainment, I ask him if the corpse is fresh, but he's not sure.

As I was crawling around, the dressing came off my elbow. I throw it away, noticing the wound is almost completely healed. In the evening a messenger arrives, bringing food and water and a few hand grenades. Dusk falls. This time too it stays quite bright in the night, as all the burning houses along Długa Street and the Krasiński Square cast a red light over us. In the distance we hear the perpetual rumble of artillery. It must be the Russian front. The sound lifts our spirits. They're so near! When will they finally arrive?

18 August 1944

At one point I become aware that the gunfire along the front line is intensifying. Usually at night, we hear bursts of fire from individual machine guns behind the German lines and occasionally one or two rifle shots. Now the fire from all the machine guns blends together, along with short bursts from machine pistols and occasional explosions from hand grenades. It started from quite far away, I reckon from around the City Hall Palace and the Bank of Poland, but soon gets closer. Out to the left, in the park, there are flashes of tracer fire and even some voices can be heard.

I try to shake off the overwhelming tiredness and strain to listen out into the darkness of the ghetto, the most exposed of our three sides. The others start firing single shots towards any noise they hear, be it broken twigs or the sound of movement. I call over to them to save ammunition because supplies are running low.

A few times I hear things close by, but can't make out which direction they're coming from. After several minutes everything quietens down, starting with the machine pistols and the grenades. The heavy machine guns carry on for a while, but even they die down eventually. By the sound of it our side came under a German attack, which must have been repelled, because the noise of gunfire from our positions appears to remain the same.

Once again I can hear the rumble of distant artillery, which seems to be getting closer with every second. I know it's an illusion, because it sounded just the same on the night at the start of the Uprising.

The dusk is beginning to fall when suddenly more gunfire can be heard, this time coming from right behind us. One machine pistol is firing very long bursts and a few rifle shots respond. Then I hear footsteps running down the street behind us. I grip my rifle tightly but am not quite sure what to do. Whoever it is is very close. A silhouette flashes past the window. A hand grenade explodes suddenly. 'Pik', the previous night's excitement still fresh in his mind, threw a grenade from upstairs. I fire a few times without taking aim. Silence.

We wait a few moments but nothing happens. We start getting agitated because 'Baszkir' reckons we've shot one of ours. I'm not so sure myself. None of our soldiers would come running down the street. If anyone of ours was making his way towards us, he'd have done so through the cellars. We'll just have to wait till daylight to sort it out.

In the pale light at dawn I'm lying in the rubble on the first floor looking out onto the street. 'Baszkir' nudges me, pointing to a shadow lying on the pavement. It looks like a body. We sneak out into the park, crawling along on our bellies under the shelter of the wall. From the first floor 'Pik' keeps his rifle trained on the fallen figure, as you can never be too certain what may happen. The wall dividing the park from the street is no more than half a metre high. There used to be a railing running along the top of it before the Germans stole it for scrap metal. It's easy enough to crawl along the wall, the only problem how to get over it. On the other side there's an open street with no cover from the machine-gun nest, which I know only too well from the time we attacked the Stawki.

Eventually, we decide to peek through a hole where the wall has been partly destroyed by a tank shell. On the sidewalk, lying face down in a pool of blood, lies a young man. He's dead – that much is obvious. He's bare headed, dressed in army issue trousers and a jacket. Lying next to him is an MP40, hanging round his neck by a sling. If I stretch out my hand I can grab his foot. I do so and start to drag him closer. Two of us pull as gently as we can, shaking with fear lest we provoke a burst of fire from the bunker at the end of the road. Eventually, we managed to drag him close enough for me to undo his ammunition pouches. A moment later 'Baszkir' takes his sub-machine gun. Ignoring the blood, I run my hands over his pockets to see if there are any papers on him, but there are none. On his wrist is a large watch, probably gold. We leave it, it's not for us.

We crawl back to our position and examine the weapon. It's virtually new. The unusual thing is that both the weapon and the spare magazines are completely empty.

A little later 'Mors' arrives, and explains what happened. He was standing by the barricade next to the square, when he noticed two people climbing over towards the Germans. They refused to stop so he opened fire. That had been his MP40 that we heard. One of them fell, dead, but the other had made it as far as us. It's obvious, now, they were snipers returning to their positions after using up all their ammunition. I, at least, benefited from a new pair of boots to replace the ones cut in two by a grenade fragment in the ghetto.

Around midday 'Jeremi' himself, the battalion commander, came to visit. He inspected our positions, looked out into the garden, but when I asked him about any chance of us being relieved, couldn't promise anything. The battalion is very short of men: we are running at about one third strength compared to when the attacks first started in Wola. Every man is permanently on guard.

I start to worry about the coming night, our fourth without sleep. I can't allow anyone to fall asleep at their position. Whilst it's still light I decide we should all take turns to sleep two hours at a time. The one whose turn it is can sleep on the floor next to his position, fully dressed with weapon at the ready, so that at the first sign of trouble he can be woken up with a kick.

The day drags on without mishap. The German Stuka dive bombers take advantage of the weather. Every now and then we hear them, droning above us. Sometimes we can see a silhouette through a hole in the roof. The bombs slung beneath the fuselage look quite menacing. Soon after a scream of the diving aircraft not far away can be heard, followed by the whistle of the bomb and the dull thud as it explodes.

As it gets dark we all take up our positions once more. There are just enough of us to have one person looking out in each direction from where danger could come. As I expected, two hours of sleep have made no difference, and the fight to keep our eyes open becomes harder and harder. We try all sorts of ways to stay awake, none of which is particularly effective. Propping up your eyelids with matchsticks causes such intense pain that you have to take them out after a while. Once you do, the eyelids come down, and it takes a super human effort to lift them up again. Pouring water from our canisters directly into our open eyes does have some effect though. A few times I find myself on the verge of unconsciousness. I see that my friends are going through the same torment. Every time the gunfire dies away, we can hear the sound of Russian artillery in the distance.

19 August 1944
Fortunately, the Germans didn't try anything last night, but I couldn't swear if one of the boys didn't doze off for a second or two. At one point a shot broke out somewhere nearby, answered quickly by a burst of sub-machine-gun fire from our positions. I'm not sure whether a semi-conscious sentry pulled a trigger by accident, or whether he indeed saw something.

The light of day brings some relief from the constant battle with sleep but its ghost is never far away. It's impossible to think of anything, or talk about anything else, only sleep, sleep and sleep!

When the sun is high in the sky, light gusts of wind bring a heavy, sickly stench from the garden. It's the corpses. There are quite a few lying unburied nearby, particularly in the ghetto from the time of that unforgettable attack. The messenger who brings us something to eat around midday says the stink is beyond belief and wonders how on earth we can tolerate it. We just got used to it, I guess.

'Zabawa' comes to visit. A thoroughly solid individual, he stays chatting with us for quite a while. We begin to feel much better in ourselves. He also gives one of those English anti-sleep tablets to each. We're very grateful to him, especially when he leaves with me one more for each of us on his way out.

After he's gone we feel much more cheerful. We strengthen the barricades in the windows and doorways so our little house becomes a small fortress. On the down side today, the mortars have altered their range, and the shells are coming down quite close to us now. As long as we're under a roof even the closest explosions won't do us much harm. My position by the window is just under such cover, but at the back of the room there's a pile of rubble where you can see the sky. We just have to hope for the best, that nothing comes in that way, because we wouldn't be able to do anything about it.

After dark, I hand out the rest of the pills to the boys hoping we make it through this night, our fifth in a row. During the night, as usual, furtive movements out in the park can be heard. I imagine the Germans are putting their feelers out and patrolling the gardens under the cover of darkness.

Suddenly we all feel full of energy, so I decide to send out a small expedition to figure out what's going on around us. During the quietest and darkest moment, I crawl out into the garden in front of the house along with 'Pik'. We get to the place where the dead German is lying. We can clearly see his bloated abdomen. His corpse stench washes over us.

We lie for quite a while in the darkness, listening, trying to calm our nerves. Not far away in the darkness we can hear some activity. It sounds like someone digging, also hushed voices. A twig breaks and someone is walking through the bushes nearby. I can see 'Pik' getting ready to fire. In the dim light I can see his weapon shaking with tension. I put my hand on his shoulder to prevent an unnecessary gunfight. We are completely unprotected here so it's best not to indulge in pointless shooting. We are unlikely to hit anyone in the darkness, and might stop a bullet ourselves. Also it's a waste of ammunition. We crawl back to the house.

20 August 1944
Fatigue returns with a vengeance. There is a loud humming in my ears, shapes float in front of my eyes. The others feel the same way.

We take it in turns again to sleep two hours each. It's only right I should be the last, and simply can't wait for my turn. The previous five days and nights without proper rest weigh down heavily on each of us.

Somebody's clambering through the cellar. We hear voices and the rattling of weapons. 'Lot' pokes his head out from the hole in the floor, and behind him come three more people. Relief at last! I can hardly make my own words out as I hand over the position. We're free to go to the rear.

The way back through the ruins is under fire right now, but we don't pay it much attention. All we can think of is a quiet corner where we can lie down, curl up and sleep, sleep, sleep. Dust and smoke from recent explosions is billowing round the ruins of the palace. We run blindly through the darkness, which luckily gives us cover as the gunfire is so heavy you have to dive under every open window to avoid getting hit.

The quarters in the basement of the High Court are practically empty. There is somebody lying on some scattered papers in the corner. Without a second glance, I take off my helmet and lie down next to him. Then I recognise 'Bohun'.

'What? Are you better already? How's the head?'

'Not too bad, I can handle it. The hospital was so awful I applied to come back to the front.'

I ask about others from our squad. 'Zorian' and 'Butrym' are apparently much better, as are 'Gryf' and 'Lis' in a hospital near the market. It's quite far but I promise myself to visit them just as soon as possible. We don't know the whereabouts of 'Sławek' or 'Kruk'. They were last seen going into action to secure the PWPW (the State Mint Building). They must have stayed there. I wonder what state they're in, alive or dead. The latter would be terrible. I look over at the two boys lying nearby – all that's left from our squad – and think to myself that it's turned out very differently from what I expected. We all knew there would be dead and wounded, but not this blood bath. I wonder how much responsibility for this is mine, but frankly my 'leadership' counts for next to nothing these days.

Fatigue overtakes these morbid thoughts and I fall asleep.

'Get up! Get up! Get ready!'

Someone's tugging at my uniform. Slowly, I open my eyes and come to my senses. It's the middle of the night. The usual glow of burning buildings comes through the window and the rattle of machine guns from the front line. I look at my watch: I've slept nearly ten hours. I feel much better, although my head is still buzzing.

It doesn't take me long to get ready. I tighten my belt, put my helmet on, load a magazine into my weapon and I'm done. On my way out, someone presses half a loaf of bread into my hand. We're going to relieve the positions in the ghetto.

The night is misty and cold. The sky is illuminated by rockets above, and burning buildings, somewhere on the other side of the square, below. We move out into the ghetto, slipping on the loose piles of bricks as we go.

'Keep quiet!' says 'Mors', who is in charge of our small group. 'Keep it down, because if the Germans hear us, they'll start up with the mortars.'

Half of us wait our turn in the deep gully, which was probably once a courtyard of a house. The rest, led by 'Mors', disappear into the darkness. One by one, white flare rockets climb into the sky from the German positions. There's no need to fall down because they can't see us anyway. One of the rockets lands, still hissing, so close that if I hadn't moved to one side it would have landed on my helmet.

Eventually it's my turn. I take advantage of a moment of darkness and scramble up the steep sides of the gully. At the top, a figure rises up out of a shallow dip ahead of me and moves on. I slide into his place. The situation is clear, there's no need for words. Stretching out in front of the piles of rubble that make up our front line, lies the vast expanse of the ghetto. Rockets fly in shallow arcs across the sky, either one by one, or at times, a whole series of them.

After only half an hour I get a cramp in my arm, then in my leg and start getting very uncomfortable. Every brick I'm lying on feels as if it's sticking upright. I start to 'tidy up the place' to ensure maximum comfort. Painstakingly, I rearrange every brick underneath me to form a flat surface, then make a space for grenades and ammunition. Eventually, I settle down to eat something. I haven't had anything since the morning, so the bread and lemonade taste better than usual.

21 August 1944

The mortar bombs, which rain down constantly onto the Krasiński Palace and the surrounding areas, occasionally fall short and explode nearby. Shrapnel whistles close by overhead, so I set about improving my position. I dig down into the rubble with my bare hands, trying to make sure the bricks I dig up don't alter the outward appearance of my position. I have to be very quiet, and pause every time a rocket flies overhead, so it's nearly dawn by the time I have provided myself with reasonable protection. My foxhole is now over half a metre deep, with an entrance invisible from the front, and a comfortable firing position facing the enemy lines. I benefit from my hard work almost immediately, when a few salvos of mortar fire land one after another among our positions. The dust and smoke is so thick it feels as if the rubble itself is on fire.

At precisely 8 o'clock, four Stuka dive bombers pay us their first visit of the day. From where I am, there is also a splendid view of the Old Town. I watch the aeroplanes circling over the rooftops looking for a target. Then, one after another, they climb into the sky before diving onto their chosen objective. Once above a building they release a long bomb, then with a shriek of engines, climb back into the sky. Now, after a slow count to six, the explosions start. Black pillars of smoke spout from the bombarded area gradually dispersed by the wind. The aeroplanes return, having circled around for a while, this time each dropping two smaller bombs. Again the ground heaves and more smoke rises above the unfortunate buildings. Even so, that's not enough for those bastards. They circle around for a third time, when they open up with their machine guns. At that moment I think of the people who were sheltering in those houses escaping out into the open, with shrapnel from the fragmentation bombs dropping on them.

The aeroplanes fly away, but it's not long before they return. I check my watch with each attack. There is always at least forty-five minutes between each raid, the difference rarely more than a few minutes. That's how long it takes them to fly to the aerodrome, reload with fuel and ammunition, and return. I memorise the numbers and letters on the fuselage of each aeroplane. They are always the same. I lie on my back and observe how they manoeuvre. The attacks are precise and clinical in their destruction. I feel quite safe where I am, but my blood runs cold at the thought of what those people must be going through not more than 200 or 300 metres away from me.

Lying here I distinctly feel the earth rocking beneath me with each explosion. Were I to stand upright, it would be a struggle to stay on my feet. There is an unpleasant moment when the aeroplanes start flying around directly above us. I can see every menacing detail: the grey/green bombs hanging underneath, the barrel of the machine gun protruding from the propeller boss. I catch a glimpse of the pilot's face through his glass canopy. I get the feeling as though he was looking directly at me. More white rockets fly from the German lines. I'm suddenly filled with terror, completely uncovered as I am from the air. I throw handfuls of dust over my uniform to try and blend into my surroundings. They fly past. I breathe a sigh of relief, until the next sound of engines coming closer. I look out: four aeroplanes are flying in formation straight towards us. I close my eyes and press myself down into the rubble. The clatter of engines and a whistle just above us ... this is it!

Silence. The aeroplanes fly over. I'm still counting. Five ... six ... nothing. Ten ... eleven ... nothing. They didn't drop their bombs! I open my eyes. Six white rockets are flying across the sky simultaneously. They've come from the German positions but are also right above us. Probably the pilots could not figure out where the target was.

There were six air raids before midday, after that I stopped counting. The smoke from the buildings burning all over the Old Town blends into one. Sometimes, it even blocks out the sun.

Right now someone is scrabbling over the bricks behind me trying to get to my position.

'Be careful, mortar bombs are still falling,' I warn.

I hear someone near the entrance to my foxhole. I see the head of Hanka, our messenger. She's trying to get to me, but is obviously not crawling low enough because a burst of machine gun bullets spatter against the bricks over my position.

'Are you alright?'

'I'm fine, I just can't get to you near enough. Hand me your helmet.'

Surprised, I take the sweaty 'pot' from my head and hand it to her. A few seconds later I get it back, full of cakes, sweets and chocolate. I see that German supplies are finally falling into good hands! I hand her my canteen. There's a pause as Hanka slides down to the bucket, which she can't carry any nearer. After a while it comes back filled with coffee. Shortly afterwards, I see her next to 'Baszkir's position nearby.

I look at my watch. I've been here eighteen hours and they promised to relieve us after eight. Ah well, too bad.

Around about 6 o'clock in the afternoon, the relief arrives. Back in the High Court, a treat is waiting for us. The prisoners have brought water and we can have a wash! The water supplies have been cut off for quite some time now, and anyway I haven't had time to wash recently. I try too remember the last time I had a wash. Definitely not in the last week. In the mirror I can see the layers of dirt from the ghetto and from all the other places I've been in.

Afterwards, and without permission as usual, I make my way through a handy window, and cross the square towards the Pamfil Restaurant. The square itself looks strange. Apart from the deeper craters from the aerial bombs, the constant mortar bombardment has left its mark. Every few metres lies a small metal star – the flights from a mortar grenade. There are also quite a few unexploded ones, although most of these have been taken away to be made into hand grenades. Also the usual burst of machine-gun fire comes my way, so I lie down, waiting for it to pass.

When I get to Pamfil, I can see straight away they've had more casualties. In a corner I can see a whole group of friends from the battalion – 'Wacuś', 'Kazik', 'Biały' – all sitting together. I squeeze my way through to 'Zorian' and hide my rifle under his bed, as weapons are forbidden here.

'Zorian' is feeling much better, and can already sit up. 'Butrym' gives me a nice surprise – he's already on his feet, although unsteady. The atmosphere here is very cordial, almost like a family gathering. Everybody's asking for news and the nurses always bring something nice to eat, which I take advantage of, as the hospital is well supplied. For my part I've brought a couple of bottles of wine some of my canny friends smuggled into the quarters, but did not hide well enough. It's pleasant sitting here chatting, and I don't feel like leaving. Deep in conversation, I fail to notice the happy brood took out my automatic rifle and started to play with it. However, it is noticed straight away by a doctor entering the room, and a small family row ensues. I realise it would be better for me to slip away quietly, so I do.

22 August 1944

The sound of explosions: one, two ... and a third. The floor of the Law Courts, where we're sleeping side by side, sways to and fro as if in a moving vehicle. Someone's helmet falls to the ground with a bang. That woke me up alright. I choke as the hot smoke fills the room. Surely we can't be on fire again? I crawl out into the corridor to get some fresh air.

The ground floor of the building is a mass of rubble. It's hard to know whether there is any more or less of it. A flickering light comes through the shattered windows. Something is burning in the square. Houses? Yes. There are also signal fires burning, to guide in the air drops. Not that they are much use, as we know by now.

I look at my watch. 3.00am. I've been asleep for five hours.

'Can't a person get any bloody sleep? I swear out loud.

A silhouette moves out of the shadows. I recognise 'Bohun'. He's standing still looking out towards the flames.

'What are you doing here?'

'I'm just standing here, I couldn't sleep.'

'What caused all that smoke?'

'Rocket launcher. Two landed here, one next door, and the rest into the square.'

'Oh.'

There's a moment's silence, interrupted by the usual nocturnal gunfire, after which I resume the conversation.

'Why can't you sleep, 'Bohun'?'

'How can I sleep ... when I know I'm going to buy it tomorrow.'

''Bohun'! Are you out of your mind?'

'I'm sure of it.'

'Give it a rest, mate. Everybody gets those feelings.'

'But its true, 'Deivir' ...'

A call from down below: 'Third platoon, wake up! Fall in!'
Our conversation interrupted, we get ready to march out.
To the ghetto again. The Germans obviously heard us coming, because we're greeted by a flurry of grenades just as we start out into the rubble. There's a whistle and a shower of sparks flies past. I fall to the ground. Somebody cries out.

'What's up?
'Nothing, just a scratch.'
We carry on. I'm in a slightly different position today, on the highest point. I'm feeling very pissed off for some reason. After a while, I'm seized with white-hot anger. I'm not quite sure why. It might be the result of my conversation with 'Bohun' or the visit to Pamfil. Looking to the rear of my position I can see in the light of the burning square the Garnizonowy church and next to it a building behind a huge pile of sandbags: Pamfil. If the Germans make it through here . . . but no, they won't come this way. I decide to somehow annoy the Germans but can't for the moment. It's dark and rounds are passing over our heads. I'll wait until daylight. Eventually dawn breaks: that's the best time for altercations, and indeed, from time to time sudden bursts of fire break out along the line. It's too light to see muzzle flashes, yet still too dark to see puffs of smoke rising from the barrel.

It's unbelievably cold, as it always is in the mornings. I'm shivering despite my warm battle dress. I stare intently into the rubble where I know the Germans are hiding. Several times there is a movement. Not yet, it's still too indistinct to waste ammunition. The sun must be coming up soon because the high ruins on the other side of the ghetto begin to shine in a pale light.

At last! Something inside me tightens up with emotion. It could be my heart, but more likely it's my stomach. I see two shadows rising up behind the enemy lines. Slowly they move to the rear. They are carrying something. Maybe a casualty? This is payback for Wola! I adjust my sights and wait for them to move into a better position. There! Bang! Bang! Bang! This automatic rifle is a fantastic weapon, ready to fire the moment the barrel comes down after the previous shot. I look carefully through the dispersing smoke. There's a dark shape lying on the rubble. Bang! Bang! Bang! The spent cartridges scatter around me. Then a loud crash just above my head. Fragments of brick come tumbling down. I huddle down at the bottom of my trench. One does not argue with a heavy machine gun. The burst hits the top and the sides of my position. The next comes right through the firing hole. Instinctively I curl my legs under me. The gunfire dies down. Carefully I place half of the binoculars into the opening and look through one eyepiece. The area I was firing into is empty. Hang on, there is something. What's that? I see a helmet lying in the rubble. Who knows ...?

The Germans have become much more cautious recently. I can't see anything worth shooting at. Apart from that ... I'm simply scared. Say what you like, but a heavy machine gun right in front is no joke. I can feel its fearsome power when the bricks around me disintegrate to dust. If I close my eyes, I can still see the German we shot at the foot of the stairs in the Blank Palace, when a mass of red jelly where his head used to be splashed all over the place. Brrrr. It sends a shiver down my spine.

Much later, I try again with a few more shots, but can't really see much to aim at. The aeroplanes fly over today, as usual. Apart from them, the rocket launchers are busier than ever. Every ten minutes or so you can hear them shrieking dreadfully, followed by a whoosh, and then explosions somewhere behind us. They don't rock the ground quite as much as the bombs dropped from the dive bombers, but instead you can feel the air compressing as they fly overhead. Roof tiles, planks and other debris fall from the roofs. All this can only be seen after the first explosion, after that, everything is covered by an impenetrable cloud of dust. After a while, I note that with every whistle passing overhead I can easily spot the actual missile. They're flying not far over our heads in groups of six, as if in formation. Their flight path is always directly over our heads. It appears that the rocket launcher is not far away. Judging from the noise it must be somewhere near Pawiak.

During one of the salvos I notice something unusual. Five missiles are flying together followed by a sixth one. It looks as if it was chasing them. Something wrong is going on. The missile starts turning somersaults in the air and is quite low. Right towards us, in fact! Here it comes! With a loud whistle the metal cylinder flashes past, falling between us and Bonifraterska Street, not further than 80 metres away. I cower down, pressing my fingers into my ears. Silence.

'What was that?' asks a voice nearby. It's our messenger, who was just on her way with our lunch.

'That? That was a dud.'

I start telling her all my observations into the behaviour of the rocket launcher. In return I get a ton of news. Sixty people buried in Długa Street. Twenty killed in Freta Street. A hospital hit on Kiliński Street, followed by a long list of other places. I suddenly realise the horrific significance of this firework display.

The bombardment doesn't ease in the slightest during the afternoon. This is new. In addition, I can hear a vicious gun fight away to the right. They must be attacking again. Things are hotting up ...

At one point, while watching the flight of the rockets, I catch my breath. They are heading straight for the cross roads between Długa and Miodowa Streets. A black cloud emerges from the corner house and a burst of yellow flame spurts in all directions from the roof of the nearby Garnizonowy church. An incendiary bomb. The church is on fire, and everything around is obscured by thick smoke. Pamfil is just next door and completely invisible in this smoke.

By a stroke of luck we're relieved just at that moment. After we return through the rubble of the palace to our quarters I break away from our group and run straight across the square to Pamfil and rush inside. Lots of noise and commotion. The wounded are lying on their beds covered in a thick layer of plaster. Everything is out of place and covered in dust. I reach the beds where 'Butrym' and 'Zorian' are lying. 'Zorian' is very pale and tries to get up from his bed.

''Deivir', 'Deivir', that was awful. We're lying here completely exposed, unable to move with everything's coming down around us. Look at that guy over there without a leg. After the first explosions he tried to get up and escape.'

'Lots of them have been blown straight out of their beds onto the floor,' adds Halszka.

''Deivir', what are we going to do? We're so exposed here on the ground floor. During the explosions, it looked as if the ceiling was coming down any minute.'

I reassure them as best I can. The building is strong. It won't fall down. They won't be firing this way any more ... I don't believe the words even as they come out of my mouth. The building does in fact look quite strong with arched ceilings because it used to be a posh restaurant, still it's not the same as being in the cellars. Apart from that I saw the Germans aiming in this direction, directly at the church tower.

What to do? I'm not sure myself. For the moment I move about, shifting rubble, fixing what I can. I'm just getting back to 'Zorian's bed when there is a piercing shriek of the rocket launcher. Complete panic ensues. Someone gets up shouting. I'm about to say 'I'm sure it's not for us,' when already I can hear the whistle of incoming rockets. There's an ear splitting explosion. Something knocks me to the ground. Instantly it becomes as dark as if we were in a cellar. My first thought – we've been buried. I jump up and take a step in the darkness with my arms stretched out in front of me. A blinding flash. Then another, and another. I'm thrown onto a bed. Somebody grabs my hand convulsively. I think to myself: so this is death. I want to shout: 'Don't worry 'Zorian'', but am overcome by the stinking, choking fumes.

Completely deafened, I don't hear the next explosions. The walls begin to fall down around us. Quite a lot falls on my back. I bend down, covering the wounded man, waiting for the rest to fall down. We wait. Fractions of a second seem like eternity. Everything goes quiet. Even the silence is ringing in my ears. We're buried. I suddenly realise it's not silence but a terrible mixture of cries, screams, shouting and meaningless words. I whisper to 'Zorian'. 'It's OK, don't worry. It's passed.'

'Me? I'm not worried about a thing.'

In the darkness I see a point of light and make out an outline of something lighter. It's a window. The sandbags have been blown away, and it has partially collapsed inwards. I realise now that we're not buried. It's just the smoke shutting out all the light. Slowly it settles. The hall is a mess of wounded and non-wounded, beds and equipment. Someone is moaning terribly, others are calling for help. Under the window someone lies dead, either from shrapnel or falling rubble. Torn dressings lie everywhere and blood seeps from fresh wounds. There are deep cracks in the ceiling, in one corner it's about to fall in. In fact, the whole structure looks as if it might come down on those lying beneath any moment. Everything is black and charred. I notice my hands, which I held in front of me during the second explosion, are completely black, but only on the back.

The entrance to the rear of the hospital is blocked by the wounded who could still walk, escaping outside. A doctor rushes into the hall, and carries out the first wounded he sees in his arms. I try to lift 'Zorian', but each effort provokes intense pain in his shattered body.

'' Deivir' you won't manage. Get some help and a stretcher.'

I realise it's the only way. I jump over the bodies lying on the ground and crawl across the fallen rubble and sandbags by the exit into the open square. Our umbrella, torn to pieces by the flying shrapnel, is still hanging on the partially destroyed buildings of the High Court in the distance. I run across the square towards it.

I make it to the colonnade, when the rocket launcher shrieks again. I take cover behind the nearest column. A loud whistle, followed by more explosions. I don't dare to lift my head from under my helmet but can hear only too well from which direction the explosions are coming. One last bang. A cloud of smoke rolls over and covers me. I lift myself up on my elbows and strain my eyes towards Pamfil. Slowly the contours of the buildings on the other side of the square unfold. The church. The tenements. The broken wall. Jagged ruins protruding from the first floor. Rubble spilling out onto the street from the gap where the entrance used to be, bristling with broken beams.

I am terribly tired all of a sudden.

I lower myself down again on to the pavement and lie still.

23 August 1944

I've been standing guard at my position in the ghetto since yesterday evening. We occupied this position unexpectedly after repelling a German attack at dusk. There was a ferocious exchange of gunfire and explosions of hand grenades. By the time we got there to help it was all over. We lost one man dead and another wounded. It's hard to estimate losses on the German side, but there were definitely a few killed, and we captured a Dreiser machine gun.

All of us were called up to reinforce the position overnight. I lie in a hollow with 'Rebe' but nothing much happened all night. This morning 'Rebe' disappeared, but I'm still here.

The German heavy machine guns are like rabid dogs today. I inadvertently knocked over a few bricks on the outside of my fox-hole, provoking a stream of bullets which went on for several minutes. The upper part of my barricade has been pulverised into a fine powder. Bullets come flying in through the firing hole quite frequently. Fortunately, I don't need to use it anymore, as I've made two new observation slits lower down, which are well hidden. In 'Sławek's absence, our light machine gun is being fired by someone from the first platoon. Then a bullet got in the underside of the cooling jacket, so it's been taken away, back to the armourer.

The Stuka dive bombers also pay us frequent visits. Their latest targets are the buildings on the other side of Bonifraterska Street, not more than 120 metres from us. Bombs coming away from the aircraft and landing in the depths of the building can be seen all too clearly. Chunks of wall and floorboards fly in all directions. Quite a few have landed near us. After one explosion I thought I saw a human body flying through the air, but it might have been an illusion.

I am terribly tired, suffering from lack of food and sleep. Every few minutes I look at my watch, as though I was due to be relieved at some particular time. I try not to think about anything, just look through my tiny opening at the area in front of me or I turn around and look behind me at the ruins around Krasiński Square and beyond into the Old Town, shrouded in thick clouds of smoke.

I hear crunching of boots along the path that runs along the gully between piles of rubble. I'm being relieved. Someone crawls up to my position. It's 'Bohun'. He looks very disheartened, nothing like the spirited young man of the few weeks ago, who was constantly urging me to get involved in the action. His face is caked in dust, eyes are red from lack of sleep, a filthy bandage protrudes from under his helmet. I crawl out backwards to give him room.

'Grenades are in the same place as before. Nothing else has changed but be careful, they're really hammering us today.'

'Right.'

I slide down the rubble. Back in the High Court, our quarters are quiet which means – everybody's asleep.

' '"Baszkir", what did you do with that tin of meat we were going to take to the hospital? We might as well eat it ourselves now.'

We open the can with a bayonet, one of the better ones. There used to be lots of them at the beginning, but they're coming to an end now.

Somebody sticks his head through the window.

'Two volunteers to bring a casualty from the ghetto!'

'Baszkir' gets up. I can't go with him as I can't carry heavy weights with my arm yet. After a while, out of interest, I get up to see who's been wounded this time. 'Baszkir' and another lad are coming through the rubble of the palace, carrying someone on a stretcher. Difficult to recognise who it is, as his face is covered in blood. A red and white mess spills out onto the canvas of the stretcher from the back of the head. Suddenly, I notice a lock of curly blonde hair which had not been matted with blood. It's 'Bohun'!

I follow the stretcher into the dressing station. Our battalion doctor arrives. He looks at the wound and shakes his head.

'The bullet entered through the jaw and came out through the back of his head. He won't live more than fifteen minutes.' He straightens up and walks over to another casualty. 'Baszkir' and I stand beside the stretcher, unable to say a word. 'Baszkir' and 'Bohun' were best friends.

Suddenly 'Bohun' stirs and starts to moan quietly. It's obvious he's suffering terribly.

After a while I burst out, 'Please, doctor, maybe we can do something? Maybe a dressing ...'

'I've already told you it's hopeless. He'll be dead in less than half an hour and we don't have many dressings.'

He goes back to his work. We sit on either side of the stretcher. The moans of the wounded boy get louder and louder. He starts crying out some incoherent words. A few times I hear my pseudonym. He starts to shout and scream with pain. I can't look at his head or what's coming out of it onto the stretcher. I turn away. His cries tear at me until I feel about to pass out. In the end I get up and run out of the hall.

Once behind the doors I start to feel terribly ashamed. How could I abandon a friend like that? How low can you get? I turn to go back, but each time a louder shriek forces me back and I can't bring myself to return.

After a while the doors open and 'Baszkir' comes out. He doesn't look up. 'He's unconscious,' he mutters. We pace up and down by the doors of the ward. The screams get louder and louder. I can't stand it any longer and move away from the doors. The sound of his screams follow me right down the corridors, right down into the furthest reaches of the ruins. I go down into the basement. I see 'Baszkir' lying in the corner with his face hidden in a pile of old uniforms, sobbing. I escape out into the street. I wander around not knowing or caring where I'm going. A few times I blunder aimlessly into some crossfire. Eventually I return to the court buildings where I find 'Baszkir'.

'It's all over.'

A long moment of silence. Eventually, 'Baszkir' stirs.

'We're the only two left from the whole squad, 'Deivir'. We have to look after each other.'[10]

It's true. I finally have to admit to myself our group of ten that knew each other so well, no longer exists. I believe the same thought is going through both our minds: Who's next? But neither of us says a word.

24 August 1944

Our quarters feel a bit empty now. The gramophone no longer bellows, and the few amateurs who were unenthusiastically cheering themselves up from a 100 litre barrel of wine standing in the corner, were knocked out by a mortar in the palace yesterday. Rucksacks and various pieces of equipment which belonged to the dead and the wounded are scattered everywhere. I've just heard that 'Mors' was wounded in the ghetto yesterday. And so there's only four of us left from the entire platoon as 'Piechocki' has been sent to headquarters to act as a messenger. We are no longer divided into squads or platoons, and 'Lot' is in command of what remains of the third company. There are now just over twenty of us left and that includes the drivers from the motorised group.

In the morning we buried 'Bohun' and one other in the courtyard. Shells were landing all around us more than usual. 'Baszkir' and I

[10] They didn't know if 'Sławek' was alive.

worked up quite a sweat 'encouraging' the German prisoners who were digging the grave.

We were just returning back to our quarters down the stairs when something exploded with a loud bang above our heads. In the darkness and smoke that usually follows those explosions, I manage to crawl into a small niche on the staircase. The rubble comes down with a huge crash. I feel my legs being buried under piles of bricks. Fortunately, they're only falling under their own weight. When the dust clears, I observe we have a new window, two storeys high. Judging by its size, I reckon it must have been a 220mm shell that hit us.

At around 9 o'clock the gunfire around the frontline intensifies. As usual in such cases, there's an immediate alert. We run towards the palace fastening our belts and webbing as we go. I'm in an awkward situation as, after yesterday's gunfight in the ghetto and having lent forty bullets to somebody, I now have only two magazines and a handful of loose rounds left. There's very little chance of me getting any more ammunition, especially not now, just as I'm running into action.

It seems that fortune smiles on the stupid, though. Running through the burnt out ruins of the palace I see two people I have not met before, leaning over a box, dragging shiny belts of Dreiser ammunition out along the floor. There's not much time, and without a word I crouch down next to them and help dismantle the belts. Soon after, I run out after the rest of the company with my backpack and pockets stuffed full.

The gunfire in the rubble behind the palace is deafening. Just above me our light machine gun is banging away without stopping.

'Where's the third company?' I shout to someone, trying to make myself heard above the noise. He waves his hand towards the High Court building. Good. At least we're not in the ghetto this time, I think to myself, as I rush down the stairs. The building is very badly damaged, rubble is piled up everywhere. The situation is clear, so I don't need to ask anyone for instructions. I run up to the second floor, climb over shattered furniture and broken fragments of wall, and soon find myself a firing position overlooking the ghetto.

What I see amazes, and at the same time terrifies me. I see a perfectly executed German infantry advance across the ruins of the ghetto. Like clockwork, they run, fall to the ground, take cover, run again, in the general direction of the St John the Baptist hospital to one side of us. Dust and smoke is everywhere, so thick it occasionally blocks our line of sight.

There's no time for reflection. I pull back the bolt, load a round into the breach and check my sights. I spot one Nazi leaping up. I see where he's hidden. Bam! Bam! Bam!

'You idiot, not too fast,' I scold myself, 'or they'll wipe you out.'

It's difficult to control myself every time I see something deserving a bullet. I don't stop until I've emptied both my magazines and start loading them again. 'Slowly, slowly,' I keep telling myself. 'Take it easy, or they'll think you're a machine-gun nest.'

I didn't need to wait long. Bullets from a machine gun splatter around the opening from which I'm firing, reminding me how important it is to change positions frequently.

As I crawl around, I realise we are not the only ones doing the shooting. German bullets crash into the walls, ricochets whistle around the room, plaster falls from the ceiling. Long ribbons of smoke from tracer bullets stretch across the sky and disperse quickly.

I find an excellent position in the second row of rooms. From the broken doorway of the outer room and through the hole in the outside of the building, I can fire outwards with little chance of being spotted. I drag up a table and, lying down on top of it, start firing. The Germans begin to leap closer and closer. They're already quite near the hospital and also us. Seen from here, the hospital and the barricade to one side appear deserted, all that can be seen is a little spurt of dust each time a bullet hits a wall. The defenders are keeping out of sight, but you can tell their presence by the fact that the German attack has somehow come to a halt. In some places you can even see them hopping back over the rubble. I've cleaned my rifle carefully. It's firing smoothly now with the fresh ammunition. There's no lack of targets but obviously it's hard to tell how successful I've been.

I change positions. I can smell burning wood. It takes me a while to realise where it's coming from. The blue smoke rising up in front of me is coming not only from the breech but also from the wooden parts of my rifle. The barrel is now so hot it's marking the rest of the rifle black!

I cease firing and move once again to another position. The first line of the German attack has stopped advancing for some reason. On the other hand, there's quite a commotion around the buildings near Muranowska Street. I set my sights on 500 metres and start firing slowly and carefully. I can see the Germans taking their wounded to the rear on stretchers and supporting them. There's also lots of people running around, either messengers or carrying boxes, probably with ammunition.

Bam! Bam! Bam!

Shit! I've been spotted!

A burst of machine-gun fire crashes in right next to me. The ricochets fly to one side. That was a bit of luck. I return to my original position lying on the table.

I see something in the distance moving around in the ghetto. A cloud of dust. I put my rifle to one side, and reach for my binoculars. I see nothing. I clean the lenses ... There! A tank! I see the turret moving between the piles of rubble. It drives out into the open, now visible in all its splendour. A feeling, not so much fear as a strange emotion, sweeps over me. I see grenadiers huddled beside the tank. I lay down my binoculars and raise my rifle again. The strange feeling brought on by the sight of the tank in the six-fold magnification of the binoculars passes. I check my range. I would have to set my sights on 600 metres. Why bother? There are better targets closer.

Bam! Bam! Bam! Nothing moves.

I look back towards the tank. It's labouring heavily over the uneven ground. What is worse is, it's not alone. Behind it appears a second, then a third. Between the shots I can hear the sound of their massive engines straining. They're making their way along the wide street where our attack failed not long ago. The wagons are still on the rails running down the middle of the road. The leading tank gathers momentum, drives up on top of the first wagon and halts. I didn't expect that. The tank reverses, builds up speed, smashes into the wagons, climbs on top and halts again. The steel skip buckles and comes off the rails. The tank stands almost vertical but the chains joining the carriages together hold fast. With a scream of engines reaching as far as us, it gives up, reverses to drive the long way round, followed by the other tanks. I admit I found myself staring at this unusual sight and for a moment forgot where I was. The tanks advanced to the point where I know their grenadiers are lying. Another tank joins them from the rear and together they make their way through the rubble in single file, heading towards the hospital. They're now quite close. I recognise them now as the massive Tiger tanks, misshapen by the addition of steel plates to deflect anti-tank weapons.

They come to a halt. The huge turrets rotate slowly and lower their huge cannons. I begin to feel a bit unwell, and fire at the arrogant bastard hiding behind the body of the nearest tank.

The unpleasant moment of the muzzle of the cannon pointing directly at me, has gone. The tanks start firing into the hospital at a range no more than 150 metres. Flames leap from the muzzles. Again and again, jerking backwards after each shot. The tanks are shrouded in dense smoke, which makes it difficult for me to pick out the Germans now acting with confidence. However, I too, having realised they are not firing at me for the time being, am not saving my ammunition.

After each shot from the tanks I see rubble and pieces of wood falling away from the hospital building and the barricade in front of it. In a few places fire breaks out and thick smoke obscures the view. Generally, there's so much smoke and dust around that it's difficult to see anything, nevertheless I fire at anything that moves.

The nearest tank stops firing. The massive tracks start to rotate and it moves slowly in my direction. I hold my breath. The Tiger is now so close I can see every detail, even the mud splattered over the armour plating. It comes to a halt so close to the mound in the ghetto where I had my position that it could have easily been reached with the heaviest grenade. Yet from the position there nothing moves. It must have been abandoned or the person there has no anti-tank grenades, or else he's dead.

The tank turns on the spot and opens fire towards the hospital. Something moves in the distance. I can see two more tanks coming. They appear somewhat different, smaller. Goliaths? Probably not, they're too big for that. One of them doesn't manage to get over the rubble of the ghetto, the other disappears out of sight in the thick smoke.

I hear footsteps running through the neighbouring room, and take a look. Someone is dragging a PIAT along the floor, followed by a girl carrying cardboard tubes containing the rounds for it.

'Over here, over here!' I shout in their direction, and move away from my position. 'There's a good view from here.'

The building is rocked by an explosion.

'They're shooting at us. Hurry, hurry!'

I help him set up the PIAT.

More explosions. I look out for a split second and see the tank firing directly at us. The shells land underneath us and to the right. I can smell the explosions. My colleague aims the PIAT. At that moment I notice the round in the barrel has not been primed.

'Stop, stop!' He looks at me.

'You've forgotten the primer.'

I can see he's a bit over excited as he's only just arrived on the front line. I grab the PIAT away from him and fit the primer. I press the heavy weapon into my shoulder. The tank is in front of me, as if on a plate. I can see the enormous armour plating and the smoke coming from its muzzle. I set my sights. Slowly ... carefully ...

The tank fires, below us again. I aim just behind the turret. There! I squeeze the trigger. The PIAT recoils, the round flies through the air ... nearly there ... It misses the tank and explodes to the rear of it. 'F***!'

Now my colleague tears the PIAT out of my hands. I don't stop him. I load a new round. Two more shots from the tank. Presumably they haven't noticed us. Suddenly it dawns on me – we're on the second floor!

'Aim lower, much lower, under the tracks. We're too high up here.'

The barrel of the PIAT tilts down. I'm oblivious to everything, glued to the gap in the wall. The weapon barks. There's a flash of light against the side of the tank.

Got him! The tank is momentarily covered in smoke. There's a flash and an explosion nearby.

'Run for it, they're going to fire!'

We run towards the exit. Shell after shell fires into the room. Everything is covered in a thick white dust. We sprint down the stairs three at a time.

Suddenly the lad running in front of me stops. A jagged abyss where the stairs used to be yawns through the smoke.

'Back!'

We run up to the half landing and along the length of the building towards the other staircase. Eventually we reach the ground floor next to the viaduct. It's safer here. I stop to catch my breath. It all took place over a matter of minutes, but it seems to me as if several hours have passed. Above us there is explosion after explosion and the crash of falling rubble. A few times I try to get back upstairs but I'm driven back by the proximity of the blasts.

It quietens down a bit. I leave my window on the ground floor from where nothing can be seen anyway, and return upstairs. The first thing I see is 'our' tank and another standing next to it. Behind it, there's another tank reversing. I don't see any infantry, at least none nearby. I look closely at the tank we hit. I can't see any great damage, on the other hand it is leaning to one side.

Then ... Oh hell! The motor of the second tank roars with all its strength. Both start moving. One is dragging the other. They're moving off now. They are already beyond range. Now they're on the street and moving away into the distance out of sight. F***!

My old position is covered in a metre of rubble so I settle down elsewhere. I resume my usual hunt for the Germans who occasionally show themselves. A rocket launcher shrieks nearby. With each explosion I notice how the swaying walls of the building separate here and there for a few centimetres and then come together again. I don't get the feeling of being well protected in this building, especially when I consider the viaduct underneath us. With every explosion I wait for the walls to fall down but nothing like that happens.

Night falls.

Nothing new to write about, just the usual rockets, the usual burning houses nearby, the usual colourful streaks of tracer fire over the ghetto.

25 August 1944

A pleasant surprise today. 'Gryf' has left hospital. As it turns out, ever since I returned to action the last time, I've never managed to get away further than Pamfil, so I didn't even know if he was alive or if he too was buried in the rubble. We have some free time before noon, so the two of us spend it together as the 'whole squad'.

We decide to visit 'Jacek'. It took a fair amount of time searching amongst the ruined houses on Długa Street. Eventually we find a hole in the ground, which calls itself a section of some hospital or other. It consists of two cellars under a ruined building. It's completely dark, illuminated only by several stubs of candles. There's an unbelievable stench of rotting wounds inside. It's packed with casualties, squashed together side by side.

We find 'Jacek' on a filthy litter in the middle of the cellar. He is lying between two others. One is moaning and shrieking incessantly, the other lies still but oozing horribly from dreadful burns covering his entire body. In fact, we thought it was a corpse, but apparently he's still alive.

'Jacek' himself is in a pretty poor state. The wound in his lung doesn't want to heal, it's now infected and he's got a high temperature. He recognises us with difficulty but cheers up enormously. We promise to return, knowing it's virtually impossible, as we just don't know when we'll be able to get away from the front line.

On the way back I notice an interesting sign put up by the civilian commander of the district. It calls for all janitors to search carefully over the roofs and elsewhere in their buildings, and remove any body parts they find to prevent contagion. This is to do with the recent explosion of a the booby-trapped tank on Kaliński Street (it resulted in great loss of life). We wonder what this will achieve: on the front lines there are masses of corpses lying all over the place.

We arrived back just in time, called back to the front line. Again we are to stay there for the whole night – to rest at any point is virtually impossible. I feel terribly tired to the last bone in my body, even though on the whole we're not marching extensively or exerting ourselves particularly. It's just that these twelve hours minimum stays at our positions in a high state of alertness are very exhausting.

We're in the same positions as before, in other words at the edge of the High Court looking out onto the ghetto and Bonifraterska Street. The night passes relatively uneventfully apart from a minor argument with a rather impudent German patrol. A few grenades flew over to our left, we took a few pot shots at uncertain targets, and peace returned. In the square signal fires are burning in the event of an air drop, but nothing flew in for us that day.

26 August 1944

We had barely three hours of rest after returning from the front line this morning. We're ordered to fall in, then off again. We are to relieve a sector that is threatened – Simon's Passage, this time. The boys are quite tired but as we thread our way through the piles of rubble in single file they start to get more boisterous and cocksure.

Simon's Passage is a huge seven-storey building. Running through the middle is a two-storey actual passage, presently closed off by a massive barricade, reinforced with a 75mm antitank gun. We are ordered to take up positions in the upper storeys. The huge halls in the building were converted by the Germans into storerooms for various valuable items. Shelves stretching from floor to ceiling are packed with tons of various objects – bolts of cloth for suits, linen, ready-made suits, blankets and so on. The windows are reinforced with sacks, which, as it turns out, are filled with sugar cubes. Some of it has been looted, but it hasn't made much of an impression on the sheer quantity of the stuff left behind. I take advantage myself by acquiring a change of new, clean underwear. Others cram their rucksacks with various items, but I can't see anything worthwhile to take away other than sugar.

Our positions overlook Nalewki. The Germans are sitting in the ruins not more than 50 metres away from us. We look out carefully to see if one raises his head, but they're not that stupid. A few times I imagine I see something and shoot. Obviously it's difficult to tell with what result. Camouflaged German machine guns and snipers reply. In other words, typical trench warfare. They nearly took out 'Baszkir' positioned in the window next to mine, but a handy sack of sugar bore the brunt of the bullets.

I'm put in charge of a small section of five people. In the afternoon 'Lot' arrives with a number of other 'leaders'. They ask why we aren't showering the Germans with grenades. That's easy to say but no harm in trying. 'Gryf' held the record in our squad for throwing a grenade the greatest distance, so I order him to have a go. His first Mills bomb falls a good 5 metres short. Never mind. We try again this time with a German stick grenade, which is much lighter. 'Gryf' makes ready with a healthy run up right from the middle of the hall as the leaders and I look on. He pulls the pin, runs up, and throws with all his might. The grenade sails over the barricade in the window ... hits the top of the window frame, bounces back and falls on the table.

Sssssssss.

The leaders make for the door like greased lightening. 'Gryf' dives into the cupboard and I take the nearest cover available to me, under the table.

On the table I can still hear ... Sssssssssssss.

That's long enough. I press my fingers into my ears, curl up and try to make myself as small as possible. Eventually there's a crash and a cloud of white dust. I crawl out from under the table and brush myself down. Nobody's hurt, but the table's seen better days. That's enough of bright ideas for now.

That evening some of us go foraging around the back of the building for food. We are comfortably seated around an enormous jar of preserved fruit, fishing for strawberries with knitting needles, when we hear a short whistle from outside the building. Instinctively we fall to the floor. At that moment there's a blinding flash outside the window followed by a deafening explosion. Plaster comes falling down.

'Leg it, boys!' I shout, but everyone's already in the next hall.

We've barely closed the huge iron doors when there's a new explosion behind us, followed by the crash of falling cupboards and rubble.

'Bloody hell, what was that?'

'Whatever it was, it's time to leave.'

We listen for a moment as the tank rearranges furniture on the storeys above us. One thing is difficult to understand: where is he firing from? How come he's firing from the side, when in front of the building, which we are watching carefully, there's nothing to see?

Eventually everything is quiet again. We look into the hall where we were a few moments ago. It's full of rubble from the shell, which exploded inside. The first shell hit the wall just beneath the window. Thankfully it didn't penetrate the wall, which could have been unpleasant.

27 August 1944

Night-time. Complete silence. We stay by our positions, straining with our eyes to see into the shadows stretching across the ruins in front of us by the light of each passing rocket. Twenty-four hours have passed since we took up these positions and we're fighting sleep and fatigue. We whisper softly to each other from hole to hole, and strain our ears into the darkness. It will be getting light soon.

Something moves down below. I hear footsteps and some voices. I point my rifle in that direction and wait. Suddenly there's the clatter of a Sten gun. Volleys of machine-gun and rifle fire respond from all directions. Without pausing for thought, I fire a few rounds in the general direction. Several flashes light up, followed by loud yelling in German. It's not looking good: the Germans are close, virtually in the little courtyard.

'Boys! Grenades, quickly!' I shout, as I fire blindly down. The gun-fire and explosions echo deafeningly in the courtyard.

'Big grenades!' I add, unnecessarily.

Two 'Filipinki' weighing a kilo each are hurled down below. I hand 'Baszkir' a huge lump of plastic explosive richly stuffed with rusty nails. The building shakes from the blast of the huge explosions, long tongues of flame leap up from below. 'Bloody hell, what was that?' goes through my head, and at the same moment I realise those were our grenades. The result must have been excellent as screams and howls reach us between the gunfire. The sound of several German voices shouting at once comes through the unrelenting gunfire, in particular one particular voice calling out loudly.

'Hilfe, Hilfe! O mein Gott.'

'Now you're calling for God, you motherf*****!' comes a voice from the darkness to my left.

The noise dies down. I guess the Germans must have retreated. I order ceasefire to prevent wasting ammunition. The shots die down and only an occasional volley is heard from downstairs. From the German side, however, every machine gun in the sector has opened up. The cries for help from the battle ground continue. They must have really copped it.

The situation carries on until the morning. In the grey light of the morning we can see silhouettes moving around in the foreground. A few shots are fired from various places in our building. I take aim as well but suddenly hear the sound of voices calling out in Polish. From the staircase behind us somebody shouts out: 'Hold your fire, hold your fire. They're ours.'

I repeat the order and press myself up to the opening. In the growing light it's possible to make out the figures of women moving here and there, dragging heavy objects. These civilians wandering around in amongst the rubble of the square with so many muzzles pointing in their direction from both sides make a macabre sight. The women are old and young, dressed in dirty, tattered rags. They try not to look in our direction. I see them bring a stretcher and place a dead or an unconscious German on to it. I hear a voice shouting in German but can't see where it's coming from. After a while I see a helmet sticking out from behind a broken wall. I take aim carefully but before I manage to squeeze the trigger there's a volley of machine gun fire from one side and the German disappears.

A second platoon arrives around 9 o'clock to relieve us from our positions. The soldier who comes to take up my position is armed with an MP40. Seeing as he is out of effective range for a machine pistol, we agree to swap weapons until this relief is over. I fasten the magazine pouches and run down into the cellar. After looking around for a while I find a vacant space and lie down to sleep.

I don't know how long I slept before being woken up by another explosion. The noise of aircraft engines reaches here through the thick walls. At that moment the pitch changes and develops into a shriek of a diving aircraft. The situation gets unpleasant when I realise it's heading straight for us. The shriek becomes shriller still as the aircraft evens out and simultaneously I hear the whistle of a falling bomb. After a few seconds of silence everything rocks from side to side. I can hear the rubble moving somewhere above us. We've been hit!

I huddle further down into my corner and try to get back to sleep. This turns out to be hopeless, as they haven't finished with us yet. After a few more explosions peace returns, followed by a cry.

'Everybody upstairs!'

I run out after the others. It's difficult to make things out in the dust and smoke. I start to choke and tie the blue bandana we all wear around our necks, over my mouth and nose.

'Over here! Quick! There are people buried here!'

I move towards the voice and find a pile of rubble with several people frantically digging into it. I quickly start to clear the bricks from around a leg with a boot still on it where it's sticking out of the pile of stones. Next to me they're loading some bloody remains onto a stretcher. We dig as best we can, but it's difficult because the rubble is constantly shifting. After some minutes I pull out a body. Unfortunately it's an already mangled corpse.

Thanks to the solid construction, the seven-storey building hasn't collapsed completely, but it has been seriously damaged. It's hard to tell for the time being how many people we've lost, as most of them lie buried under the rubble.

We run upstairs to try and control the blaze that has broken out on the floor above. Two storerooms filled with cloth are on fire. Thick, choking smoke makes everything very difficult. We manage to prevent the fire spreading into the other rooms. The ceilings, supported by steel beams, contain the blaze, which should eventually die out. I come across a friend of the lad with whom I exchanged weapons. It turns out that 'Janek' – that was his pseudonym – perished and they haven't found his body in the rubble. And so my rifle has been lost with him.

We take up positions on the ground floor. Somehow the fire spread from the front of the building into the cellars, which are now on fire. The smoke and flames blow through the windows and the heat is such that we can't stay at the front of the building but have to retreat inside, to the next row of rooms. Standing in the doorway I can observe the foreground through the width of the premises, which was once a shop. The billowing heat is not so strong here, and the swathe of smoke and flames keeps us out of sight, whilst allowing us to look through it.

The floor under our feet starts to provide some diversity as it changes from warm to hot. The heat from the ceramic tiles starts to burn our feet, even through the thick soles of army boots. It's quite comical to see silhouettes outlined in the thickening smoke hopping from one foot to the other.

But this is no time to stand around gawping because something interesting is happening on the enemy lines. Behind the moving curtain of smoke I detect a deserted barricade to my right, perpendicular to our lines. Actually, it's no more than a long pile of rocks

2 or 3 feet high. Something is moving there. A bent over figure runs past and disappears behind the rubble. I take aim carefully with my machine pistol. Another figure runs past. I fire a short burst. Again, two more figures. I fire two more short bursts. This time it was a German running in the opposite direction. 'What's going on?' I ask myself, as I empty my magazine in that direction. I attach a fresh magazine. The little beast is firing well. The heat from the fire intensifies, my view becomes obscured by the increasing smoke. It's becoming unbearably hot. The soles of my feet are burning painfully now. I'm completely drenched in sweat, I've finished my water. No hope of getting any more.

Something is splashing behind me. I turn around to see water cascading down onto the floor of the great hall from above, probably from a ruptured water tank. It's a great opportunity to cool down my burning helmet and steaming uniform. I put my weapon to one side for a minute, and jump with both feet under the refreshing shower, only to jump even more quickly out. Yuk! What the hell was that? It's not water but something unbelievably caustic and rancid. Probably bleach or something like that. Nothing is normal in this building: barricades are made out of sugar, firing stations out of reams of paper, and there is bleach in the pipes instead of water!

I go back to my position. It's unbearably hot now, my helmet is blistering and I'd love to retreat backwards a few metres. But next to me flickers a silhouette of my mate continuing to tread on the spot in the heat and I can't be the first to back down.

I try to concentrate on the foreground. Right opposite me is a ruined one- or two-storey house. The Germans are inside it. I examine each window carefully in turn. Suddenly ... I simply can't believe my eyes: in a first floor window I see a silhouette of a German soldier almost completely exposed. It's extreme range for a machine pistol, about 50 metres, but never mind. I set my sights, take aim carefully and fire a burst. He's fallen on his face towards me! I fire another burst but in my excitement I think it went too low. The German disappears but he was definitely hit. 'Gryf', who also saw him, feels the same.

In that truly worst moment, when my head is swimming from the heat, 'Lot' arrives and takes us away from our positions on the first floor. The fire in the two halls upstairs is going out, having consumed everything flammable.

Dusk falls. We can hear savage gunfire in the park to our right. I don't know what's going on there.

28 August 1944

'Everyone from Parasol downstairs! Fall in by the gate!'

I'm hoping this is the call for us to be finally relieved and get some rest. Buoyed up by the prospect of such a nice surprise, we hurry down the stairs. The great Simon's Passage looks an absolute mess. The barricades are partially destroyed. One, made out of bundles of typing paper, is on fire. The buildings on the other side of Długa Street are also on fire so that it's almost as light as day. Somewhere in the gardens, not too far away, come vicious exchanges of fire. Every now and then a ricochet flies through the gate and whistles past my ear.

At one end a group of our soldiers, some half lying on the ground, has already gathered. The excited expressions on their faces dash any hopes of a rest period. Soon enough we get our orders: in a few minutes we're going to counter-attack. Feverishly I check my weapon and ammunition. Somebody hands out additional hand grenades. My heart beats fast as I load the best magazine into my weapon. 'Lot' hands out instructions quietly.

The instructions are simple. Too simple for my liking. We're to reach our objective, known as the white house, in one movement. Next we're to throw grenades through the windows and occupy it. In the bright light of the burning buildings, none of this strikes me as very pleasant. Then comes the rather grim order: 'Machine pistols first!'

I step forward along with a few others. My stomach is churning. It takes all my strength to quell my rising fear. The area in front of us, brightly illuminated by the flickering light and echoing with the sound of nearby gunfire, looks most uninviting. A few moments pass and I manage to get a grip on myself. I feel calm now and waiting for the order: 'Forward! Attack!' But nothing like this happens. My nerves start jangling again. Everybody's muttering to themselves: 'Come on, come on.' What will be, will be. Just get a move on.

'Lot' comes running up. This is it! I grip my machine pistol with all my strength and prepare to leap forward.

'Unload your weapons! The attack's been called off.'

That was unexpected. I'm not sure whether to laugh or cry. Either way, we're going 'home' for a rest and that's the main thing.

We head back in a long column, only this time four or five stretchers bring up the rear. On them lie the remains of the dead we managed to dig out from the rubble. Back in the quarters, after our meal, there's another order: 'Everyone with a weapon outside!'

This time, however, we're not going back into the action. It's a funeral parade for our friends. They were all first rate and much loved colleagues. Amongst them is 'Gąsior' from our platoon.

We climb through a window outside. It's getting light already. Next to the other graves is a new hole, in which lie several bodies. A bottle containing papers is placed on the chest of each one. We assemble into ranks.

'Attention! Present arms!'

The bodies are covered with earth and rubble. Someone who clearly feels the ceremony was not solemn enough, gives the order, and we fire a salute from our raised weapons. A bit ragged, but still ... We disperse.

We sleep extremely well all day despite the nearby bombardment. In the early evening we move out to take up position in the ruins of the Krasiński Palace.

In the neighbouring window to mine is the heavy machine gun position. Its crew is assembled from the group of sixty or so people who managed to get to us along the sewers from Żolibórz. They are all incredibly nice people, most of them from Wileńszczyzna, outside of Warsaw. I get chatting with a sergeant who's in charge. We sat up talking the whole night. He told me about his campaigns with the partisans in Nowogród, the road from there to Kampinos, and then to us. On my part I tell him all about the Conspiracy and what's been happening in the Uprising so far. They are all undeniably brave, but don't feel very confident in the strange environment of the city. It's not surprising; for the last few years they've been in the country and in the forests. For them this is a completely different kettle of fish.

This night passes remarkably quickly. The Germans virtually leave us in peace.

29 August 1944

Gunfire breaks out not far away from all directions. I only now realise how small an area we've been forced into. In addition, we're expecting an attack on our positions at any moment, which fortunately doesn't come. The bloody Germans are firing doggedly into our positions through the bushes and from the ghetto, almost without pause. We can't engage them with gunfire due to lack of ammunition. There's no point going to our magazines for more supplies because there aren't any. Everybody has been told to do the best they can. During the night I crawled out a few metres into the foreground towards the body of one of our dead soldiers. I brought back three magazines and some ammunition for a Sten gun. I managed to swap them for magazines for an MP40, so now I have two pouches filled with spare magazines. I count my bullets. I have about 240. That will have to last me to the end. To what end, I don't know, and I don't think about it. This question nevertheless must be occupying everybody's mind because at that moment 'Baszkir' asks me: ''Deivir', when do you think this will end?'

I can think of nothing more clever, or rather, nothing less stupid, than to say: 'Well, everything must come to an end eventually.'

In the afternoon we're allowed to return to the quarters. There are a few wounded here already. Apart from them there are two characters from the motorised division, pissed out of their heads. It's disgusting to drink right now, but they seem to think that is an excellent reason for drinking. There's a row, but what's the use?

We settle down to some bread and preserves, while listening to the latest news. Someone in the corner is reading out an order, others are lying around listening. There's a long list of medals and promotions, the vast majority posthumous. Amongst others there's one for 'Zorian'. A number of my friends who have been put forward for decoration accept our congratulations looking very pissed off. Amongst us it's taken for granted that whoever gets the KW (*Krzyż Walecznych* – equivalent to a Military Medal), gets it in the neck soon afterwards. It might be coincidence but it almost always happens that way.

'Jeremi' comes to visit and we sit around singing a few songs. The atmosphere lifts slightly.

'On your feet. Fall in!'

'What now?' I think to myself. Half-heartedly, I get to my feet and straighten my uniform. My weapon and helmet are by my side so there's no problem getting myself ready to go.

It's dark now. We fall in upstairs in the vestibule. The whole 3rd Company now numbers only twenty-two people. We're going on a little excursion, this time to a section quite far away from the City Hall, where the Germans have infiltrated.

We set off. Długa Street is now barely recognisable. Houses on both sides lie in the middle of the street and as we walk along a sort of a path down the middle we need to climb at times almost to the height of the first floor. Hipoteczna Street is in similar state. A sentry standing along the way warns us to move very quietly as the Germans are pretty close and open fire at the slightest sound. It's difficult to do in an unfamiliar territory in the dark, and every few minutes someone trips over a sheet of corrugated iron from a roof, or knocks over some bricks. They make a fair amount of noise in the quiet night. We don't have to wait long for a reply: soon there's a gentle whistling from somewhere behind us, followed by explosions from a grenade launcher.

We get to Daniłowiczowska Street. We can see small flames flickering amongst the rubble in front of us, as if someone had lit candles. It's the remains of the prison building, burning to the ground. There's a smell of corpses and of something burning. The walls at the back of the City Hall are charred and stand empty. We climb inside. Not a soul. I go first as I'm supposed to be familiar with this area, but quickly realise that everything has changed dramatically since the last time I was here. We stand around for a while in the rubble until someone manages to find the entrance to the cellars. Several rough-looking men climb out from below. One of them appears to be in charge. He chats for a minute with 'Lot'. We head off in the direction pointed out to us. The Germans have occupied the front of the building and we're to throw them out.

'Baszkir' and I take up position by the windows looking out to the front, from where we are to engage fire with the enemy in the direction of the gate opposite. The rest run to the right. Soon afterwards we hear a shout, 'Hurrah!', followed by a few pistol shots. I see a few muzzle flashes in the gate on the other side. We open fire in that direction. Half way through my second magazine, the machine pistol jams quite seriously as a result of the German ammunition. I look around for a piece of wire to clear my jammed weapon. After a while I manage to clear it with the help of someone I've not met before.

At that moment they call us over. We run forwards and already from a distance we can see a bright light coming from a doorway of one of the rooms. It looks as if there is an electric bulb burning inside, which is impossible. It turns out the door frames are on fire, along with other flammable items inside the room. Fortunately, the floor is stone so the fire does not hinder our progress. In the next room we find a few people dragging huge steel filing cabinets. We help them barricade the passage leading out. We're right at the front of the building. The Germans have retreated. Further to the right, fire prevents further movement. The gunfire and grenade explosions die down all around. Only the German light machine gun in position on Teatralny Square carries on.

After a while spent at this barricade, 'Lot' orders me to take up new positions protecting the exit to the courtyard. I stand right in the courtyard next to the corner of the burnt out gateway. Above me stands the ruined spire of the tower – a memory from the first days of the Uprising. The situation is unclear. Just around the corner from where I'm standing is a gate through which an enemy light machine gun fires constantly. On the other side of the gate, hidden in a pile of rubble, is a small group of our soldiers, who got there along the left side of the courtyard. They are effectively cut off, as that side of the City Hall is completely demolished. To get round from there is impossible during the day, particularly under fire from the Germans situated in the ruins of the Blank Palace.

30 August 1944
It's almost dawn. The group on the other side get the order to retreat in my direction. They start to run over. The danger zone is not large, about 20 feet, but it has to be made under fire from a Dreiser situated about 60 feet away.

The first soldiers make it unscathed. I can barely watch as every silhouette is followed by a crashing burst of fire. Five had already passed me when the next gives out a yelp of pain. Staggering, he runs up to me. I grab hold of him and carry him towards the window of the main building. Something warm splashes onto me. I feel blood.

'What's up, mate?'

No reply. Only a gurgle from the wounded man's throat. I climb first through the window of the ground floor and pull him up after me. He stops, leans against me and falls to the floor. He continues to make such ghastly croaking noises, that the hair stands up on the back of my neck. I can't help him in this darkness so I shout behind me.

'Medic! Here, quickly! Wounded!'

The boy falls quiet. A girl medic runs up. I show her the casualty and hurriedly rush back to my old position. Climbing through the window I call behind me: 'What's wrong with him?'

'Dead. Shot through the throat.'

Two more run over. Somebody calls from the other side there's a casualty left behind. I pass the message back. After a moment a girl medic, 'Waligóra', comes running up. Her pseudonym (literally, a mountain crusher, also a name of a mountain peak) is very apt, as she is taller than me and exceptionally strong. I show her how to run to the other side. She crosses virtually upright. Perhaps it's just as well, as a burst of tracer fire passes just in front of her.

Through the open door on the other side I can see a figure moving. It is bent double under a great weight carried on its back. I guess it's the wounded man, but who would dare to run over laden down like that under heavy fire? The figure comes closer, she's just on the other side. She jumps, if you can call the painfully slow movement of a person weighed down by a heavy load jumping. I can see the bullets crashing into the pavement in a shower of sparks. A second burst. A third hits the corner of the gateway behind which I'm hiding, just as they approach. I recognise 'Waligóra'. I help her pull the wounded through the window and return to my position. One more person makes it across the gateway, and that's the lot from the other side.

The sun rises. The Germans must have appraised the situation because a few hand grenades land in the courtyard. That forces me to retreat behind the cover of a window. Here in this rather un-eventful position, because out on the flank, I spend most of the day. I look around me and recognise our former positions with difficulty. The first floor is completely burnt out, but the ceiling is still firm. The flames missed out the room where I am, largely because there's nothing left to burn inside. The ground, however, is still glowing despite stamping out the embers. If I leave them for a moment the fire comes closer and burns my feet.

After a while I spot something moving in a first floor window at the rear of the courtyard. I see a puff of smoke and a salvo of bullets comes past. They're our people! How did they get up there? In the next window a head wearing a helmet appears which I recognise as belonging to Corporal 'Kier' from the motorised section. I guess he must have a clear target as he fires time and again from his MP40. I figure they must have got a line on the Germans with the light machine gun near the gate. The benefit of surprise is soon lost and the machine gun replies loudly. I see a cloud of dust where the bullets hit the wall. Our boys disappear only to reappear shortly afterwards in another window. To my surprise the German machine gun suddenly falls silent. They must have hit them!

Throughout the whole day in my position, I had only one oppor-tunity to open fire. Towards the evening we head back home. Despite not having slept for twenty-four hours we're all in a very good mood, probably because throughout the whole operation we've lost only one dead and one wounded.

Our company returns in single file and makes quite an impression on all the scared faces of the civilians poking out here and there from behind broken walls. 'Lot' leads from the front leaning on a big, furled, black umbrella, our supposed emblem. Behind him is the huge figure of 'Długi' with a Dreiser nonchalantly slung over his shoulder, followed by the tiny figure of 'Sambo', draped in shiny ammunition belts. The rest of our mob trails behind. Somebody starts singing our Parasol song. It is quickly taken up.

On Długa Street, we're passed by a group of senior officers, amongst others Colonel 'Radosław' (senior commander of the Home

Army – K Division). They stop to admire our little group. Somebody calls out: 'Keep it up, boys!'

* * *

I'm sitting against the wall in our quarters cleaning my weapon. All around me, my friends are resting after getting back from the Town Hall. The conversation concentrates on the current topics, namely Germans inside the cathedral, the Fiat factory abandoned, St Jack's church bombarded today and so on. In the corner in the other side of the room, there's a difference of opinion as to how long we can hold out. Some reckon a week, others two days at the most.

It doesn't make much difference to me. It has little importance compared to the incredible fatigue and lack of sleep, which saturates every part of my body. I don't feel like doing anything, or thinking about anything. Nothing bothers me and I pay little attention to what's going on around me. If only I could just stretch out and sleep!

I've cleaned my weapon and magazines so I have a few moments to myself. I have spotted a comfortable place on top of a huge cupboard full of legal documents. Nobody will bother me there. I squeeze into the narrow gap full of dust. The ceiling is unpleasantly just a few centimetres above my face. A shell lands nearby and the walls rock from side to side as if they're about to topple on top of me.

'‘Deivir', get up, we have to fall in.' Somebody's tugging my leg.

'Bugger off, we've only just got back,' I mutter reluctantly, but there's no choice. I have to wake up.

'What's going on 'Baszkir'?' I ask as I climb down from my perch, noting the quarters are empty.

'Something big. We're breaking out.'

A double rank of dark figures all carrying weapons are lined up in the hall, all that's left of the 3rd Company. I fall in. All traces of sleep have gone and my mind is clear now. Everyone else is silent, you can see the gravity of the situation reflected in their faces. Only 'Lot's voice breaks the silence.

'… line of attack … approach … communicate only in whispers … torch signals …'

We pack up all our equipment and ammunition. I am only given about sixty bullets, but I now also have fourteen grenades, which weigh me down considerably. The night is very dark. To avoid getting lost once we get to the exit, we are all to hold on to a long, thick piece of string.

We set off. We cross the rubble on Długa Street once more and descend into the cellars on the other side. The place is full of civilians, their belongings block the way. We squeeze through the crush with great difficulty, then through various underground openings, twisting and turning in all directions. Sometimes up, sometimes down, all in total darkness, broken only by the occasional candle smouldering in a crack in the wall. I trip over things and bang into walls, firmly holding on to the string which steadily moves on. We stop, then start moving again. Eventually we reach our destination.

We stand still for a while. Some of us start looking around for a place to sit. Somebody lights a candle. By its light I see a long underground corridor and my colleagues sitting in a row leaning against the wall. A few metres behind us is an entrance to a cellar full of people. A short distance ahead the view is stopped by the bend of the corridor. Judging by the draughts of fresh air coming from that direction, I reckon the exit to the outside world must be there. We can hear the constant sound of gunfire through the concrete over our heads, muffled by the thick walls, echoing around the underground walls. We are directly beneath the front line.

The wait is unpleasant but everyone gladly takes advantage of a moment's rest. Somebody starts cutting up a loaf of bread, I open a tin of an excellent German paté. The water situation is less encouraging, however. The civilians nearby have not a drop to spare and we had no opportunity to stock up. Thinking along the lines of 'what's the point of saving it when we could get our heads blown off in a minute', 'Baszkir' and I finish off the rest of the wine in my water bottle. We're still thirsty.

31 August 1944

Time drags by agonisingly, hour after hour, without any change. The excitement dies away and I fall into a restless sleep.

I look at my watch: it is 2.30am. I doubt if anything will happen now, I'm sure it's been called off because it'll be light soon. I'm sharing these thoughts with my neighbour when a messenger squeezes past to the front of the queue where the leader is crouching. Immediately we hear the order being whispered down the line. 'Get ready! Wake everybody up.'

My heart is thumping hard. I load a magazine into my weapon. Minutes pass as tension rises. Orders and instructions pass up and down the line every few minutes. Our company will attack second. The 2nd Company, which will attack first, squeezes past. They disappear into the darkness.

The gunfire above us intensifies. Shouts and orders of 'Forward!' reach us down below. There's the sound of running feet and a commotion up front followed by shouts of 'Hurrah!' It's started. I pick myself up, press my helmet firmly down on my head and tighten my webbing. It will be our turn in a minute.

I hear something being dragged back. Again someone squeezes past, moaning terribly. As he brushes past me something warm drips onto my face. Yuk. The concrete above us creaks under the explosions of hand grenades. Two more people run past us. The shooting above us gets louder still. To us in the underground it sounds like a continuous deep rumble.

Our turn arrives.

'3rd company, advance!'

At first we move slowly. The exit at the front is narrow and we can only get outside one by one. Complete darkness. I shuffle forwards crouched over, holding onto the belt of my colleague in front of me. We start to move quicker and quicker, I trip up some stairs and finally feel fresh air hit my face. Some people stand on either side, giving us a helping hand upwards as we pass. Without them I would never made it up here. I am pulled by someone through a crack to the outside. There's a fair amount of noise and impossible to see a thing. Another person points me in the right direction and shouts, 'Keep moving!'

There are flashes from explosions all around me. Yellow streaks from tracer fire fly in all directions. It's difficult to get my bearings. I run a few steps, trip over something and fall. I jam my right arm painfully between my machine pistol and a brick. A voice to my right shouts, 'Shoot! Shoot over there!'

I recognise 'Zabawa's voice.

'Where? What at?'

'Over there ... on the other side ... in the windows ... Germans!'

I begin to make things out in the darkness. We are in the rubble of a burnt out building. In front of me is a gap where a window used to be. Through the gap I can make out the outlines of some walls. Something flashes. That's probably what he's on about, I think to myself. I fire a few short bursts. I see my bullets striking tiny sparks where they hit the wall. There's no question of any real target.

'Hurry, hurry! Don't you have any ammunition?'

I change my magazine and fire some longer bursts, hoping I'll hit something. Hand grenades keep falling in front of us. There's a blue flash as they explode some metres in front of us. Too far. The next ones fall quite close. I huddle down in my hollow. The explosion doesn't do me any harm. Someone calls out from one side: 'This way, this way! Keep moving!'

I start running, stumbling over the rubble. Yellow streaks come past on either side of me. I get the feeling it's impossible to make the slightest move without being hit. A couple of German small pocket grenades come flying out from behind a wall and into the air in a trail of sparks. One falls right under my feet. I jump over it quickly but in that moment it explodes, knocking me flat.

'That's not so bad,' I think to myself not feeling any pain.

No-one's shouting 'hurrah' now. Instead there are loads of cries and calls for help. A few shots come from directly in front of us. Something's moving up ahead. I see some silhouettes. Germans. My machine pistol judders frantically, firing from the hip. I've folded the stock, it's much easier that way. Once I reach the spot there's no-one, only a corpse obstructing the way ahead. A voice calls out for two people with grenades and they head off to one side. Impossible for me to go with them, so I hand over several grenades from my backpack.

To my left there's another courtyard, and the only exit to the right leads onto a corridor, along which a German machine gun is firing at close range. Two or three boys head that way. Immediately I have to help one back when he catches a bullet. Hidden behind a wall I shoot in the direction of the Germans.

I try to get my bearings. The house we're in is not badly damaged, at least part of the ceiling over the ground floor is still in place. Some of our boys have gone up there with grenades. The corridor where I am has a doorway on the other side a few metres away, in which we can take cover from the bullets.

Somebody tugs my sleeve. It's 'Jeremi'. I recognise him by the white bandage around his neck. He asks me about the way ahead, but before I could give him more details he heads out into the dangerous corridor without another word. There's a burst of fire. Amazingly they missed him. 'Jeremi' keeps walking. I call out to him: 'To the right, to the right. Into that hole!'

Finally he disappears from sight. I breathe a sigh of relief. Two more boys join me and together we jump ahead. To our surprise, the Germans at the end of the corridor are silent. They've retreated. We keep going along the ruins of the burnt out house. Our next obstacle is a fairly wide gateway with another German machine gun firing through it. The first person trying to cross is killed immediately. We stop in a narrow passageway and fire through gaps in the walls at the Germans who have set up position in the garage opposite. We're in a rather unfortunate position: the fire blazing to our left illuminates us but leaves the enemy in shadow.

I fire mainly at muzzle flashes. We can see a little better when someone from our side starts firing tracer rounds, which keep burning for a few seconds as they stick in the door frames and walls in the German positions. The Germans start throwing hand grenades towards us. These are the German pocket or 'egg' grenades, which are not very powerful. We can hear the detonators hissing and the clunk of the grenades hitting the wall behind which we're hiding. A few come through the gaps, but even though they explode 2 or 3 metres away they don't seem to make an impression other than a small shower of multicoloured sparks. I'm getting used to the bang.

The gunfire from our side intensifies as the Germans seem to have a mind to move towards us. A few times I notice them in the courtyard. The barrel of my machine pistol is burning hot. The grenades start falling thick and fast, and more of them reach their target. As the grenades roll in there's hardly time to jump to the side while firing at the same time. I'm beginning to wonder why I haven't been wounded yet. Most of my friends who were next to me have been hit and have headed back. There is now no more than two people in my vicinity.

The air shudders with new explosions heavier than those of normal grenades. Somebody shouts 'Mortars!', but they might have been bunches of grenades tied together, or mines being thrown. Jumping behind a corner of the wall someone is squatting down, huddled up against the wall. It's one of the girl messengers who brought us some more grenades. She sees me struggling to load the magazines in the dark and offers to help. I hand her all my empty magazines and a pouch with ammunition. In a moment she hands them back all fully loaded.

The crazy dance with the grenades doesn't let up for a minute. There's nothing we can do, as the Germans throwing them are hidden behind a wall. At one point I hear a grenade landing behind me. No time to jump to one side, I can only huddle down into the rubble. At the same time I see something bouncing along the bricks in my direction hissing and scattering tiny sparks. A second grenade! This one is no further than half a metre from my helmet. I grit my teeth and stick fingers in my ears. There's an explosion, followed by silence. At the same time a soft weight has landed on top of me.

For a moment I don't know what's happening. Someone is struggling on top of me, moaning. Somebody shakes me and asks me if I'm wounded. It brings me to my senses. Am I wounded? I don't feel any pain but my head is ringing and I can't gather my thoughts.

'No, no, I'm fine. Give me a minute to sort myself out.'

'Then go around the corner to the bathroom. It's safer there.'

I crawl off in that direction. The small ruined room is full of bodies lying on the floor. I sit down in a vacant space and lean against my machine pistol. I feel numb and detached. Somebody tells me that someone got badly wounded on top of me. 'Yeah? Sounds bad . . .' I gaze vacantly in front of me. Two girl medics move around in complete darkness. 'Why are there sparks flying from their dressings?' goes through my head as I fall into a daze again.

Suddenly there's a flash and an incredible bang. The smell cordite. I hear nothing and feel sharp pain on the left side of my head. What's happened? Immediately I come to my senses and become aware of my surroundings. A voice calling out reaches me as if from a great distance. 'What happened, did somebody fire?' In that moment it becomes clear. I run my hand over the machine pistol. The bolt is pulled back. I discover why it only let off one shot. The cartridge is jammed in the firing mechanism. I discover a small hole in the edge of my helmet and start to feel faint again. Three centimetres to one side and I'd have had a bullet in my brain. I curse myself for not making my weapon safe, but was barely conscious when, as I sat down against the wall, I leaned against my machine pistol. My left ear hurts like hell and I can't hear a thing.

I return to the gap where the battle still rages. A few moments ago 'Góral' caught a bullet in the hand jumping across the open gateway. He's now sitting on the other side of the gap while his friends are calling to him to jump back. It's not a large gap but as he runs across there's a flash of tracer fire and the poor guy falls. The Germans see him lying on the ground and fire into him continuously. The fire is too heavy and we watch helplessly from about 4 metres away. In any case we can't help him now. He's been hit so many times the Germans must know for sure he's only a corpse, but despite this they keep firing with tracer rounds. The uniform on the fallen boy starts burning. I can't watch this conscious barbarism on a fallen comrade and occupy myself firing at the German machine-gun nest carefully this time, as my ammunition is starting to run out.

It starts to get light. What happened to the attack? Why aren't we moving forward? Judging by the number of my friends left we must have taken heavy casualties, but where are the others? The reply comes shortly in the form of an order passed from mouth to mouth: 'Attack has failed in all sections. Occupy your present positions.'

We occupy slightly stronger positions. In the light of day the corridor, so hellish at night time, looks quite different. Grenades no longer fall from goodness only knows where. I help a machine gunner up to the top of the rubble with his weapon and carry the boxes of ammunition on my own, as our numbers have dwindled drastically in the night. We can't see much more from the first floor than we could from down below, but at that moment somebody sitting on a fragment of wall higher up still, calls over to us. Apparently he can see the Germans from there. The machine gunner climbs up the near vertical wall first. I pass him the Dreiser and start climbing up, holding onto protruding bricks and pieces of drain-pipe. I look carefully over the top. The German machine gun position is on the other side of the courtyard. Two Germans are lying by the machine gun and a third one a bit to the side. That's as much as I saw, a quick glimpse before taking immediate cover. Carefully we lift our little machine into position. My heart beats fast, hoping they won't see us too soon. Everything's ready. A burst of fire. I keep a look out. The bullet trails head straight towards the Germans. The machine gun growls with long bursts. The Germans start running around frantically, two lie motionless. I regret not being able to use my MP40, as it needs both hands to hold on. But already we've been spotted. Something thuds into the wall. I fall, rather than climb down, surrounded by flying fragments of brick.

*   *   *

I've been ordered to take up a position overlooking Długa Street. The ruins of the burnt out houses are still hot. The naked walls stick high up with gaps where the windows used to be. I kneel down with my machine pistol by one of them, in what probably used to be an entrance to a shop, and look carefully out onto the street. Nothing moves. I really don't feel very well. There is a hum in my head, something is rattling in my damaged ear and my crushed finger, full of dirt and without a dressing, has swollen to twice its normal size. But worst of all by far is the thirst, which is relentless and dominates everything else.

My spirits are lifted by the sound of someone calling me from behind. Maybe they're bringing something to drink. I leave 'Baszkir' on his own and crawl out behind the back wall. Some of my more enterprising friends have dug a hole into a cellar of a burnt out building and are pulling out bottles of Vichy mineral water. The flames didn't reach the cellar but everything inside has been thoroughly cooked. We all grab a bottle, break the neck on the nearest brick and sample the contents. It's a disgusting bitter liquid, tepid to boot, and not bearing the slightest resemblance to water. Somebody suggests we try adding some old raspberry syrup, thick with sugar of which there is also a large supply. I pour away a third of the bottle, fill it up with the syrup and with some difficulty swallow it down. In all honesty, I've not drunk anything quite so disgusting in my entire life. Nearby, someone who quenched his thirst over-enthusiastically noisily returns what he had just drunk.

I return to my position and resume the constant battle with sleep. The Germans do their bit to save us from boredom as already we hear a rumbling and three Stuka's arrive, flying low above our heads. My position is completely exposed to the open sky, allowing me to observe the aircraft circling over the ruins looking for a target. They each have just one bomb slung underneath, but of a large calibre.

The nearest German positions fire white rockets into the air. These aren't just to identify themselves, as one of them lands vertically onto the edifice of Simon's Passage on the other side of the street. A pillar of white smoke rises up into the still air where it landed. This is what the Stukas were waiting for. The first one breaks away from formation and starts diving onto the building. I've never seen an enemy aircraft in action this close before. Simon's Passage is not more than 30 metres away from me. It is possible to see every detail, every rivet on the aircraft, even some letters stencilled in yellow on the bomb. Just above the roof the bomb drops away and at the same time the aircraft levels out. A few crashes – that's when the bomb breaks through the floors. I watch it calmly having got used to air raids by now … and besides, there's nowhere to run to in any case.

Time for it to explode. I curl up behind the wall and cover my ears. Seconds pass … one … two … three. The air is split by a massive explosion. I glance up at the burnt walls, two storeys high, swaying above me. As long as they don't fall from the blast I'll be safe from the fragments. The walls oscillate to and fro like trees in a gale. Fragments fall from the top but they stay upright. Soot blown from a chimney comes straight towards me. I cover the working parts of my machine pistol as best I can against the particles.

I look out. The building over Simon's Passage is still standing, but enveloped in smoke. The second Stuka dives, another explosion follows. Everything goes black from the dust and smoke. In the darkness I can hear the screech and whistle of the next aircraft. Another blast, and at that moment something crushes on top of me knocking me to the ground. 'I'm buried' flashes through my mind.

For a while I lie motionless trying to work out what's happened. I move an arm, a leg – everything seems to work! Slowly the darkness clears. I pick myself up. Nothing seems to have changed much. Only, feeling around my helmet, I come across a deep dent. The brick responsible for it, having fallen from the top of the wall, lies in front of me.

The aeroplanes fly away. The building of Simon's Passage doesn't look particularly damaged from the outside. The bombs must have fallen some way behind it.

Forty-five minutes pass, and once more the rumble of the engines break through the general background noise of gunfire. It increases steadily, and soon the angular silhouettes flit across the sky carrying a fresh load. I watch the German rockets climbing into the air. Then one of the smoke bombs is flying straight towards me. I duck down instinctively and hear something falling. The smouldering casing is lying two steps in front of me spouting great plumes of white marker smoke. The first aircraft starts to dive. This is it! There is no time to hide.

I don't know what went through my mind during those few seconds as I was lying on the ground, not looking up, hearing the aircraft screech past, the bomb falling and silence, during which the timer of the detonator ticked slowly. Finally the explosion and the slow realisation that I'm still alive. The pilot obviously remembered where his real target was.

Somewhat shaken, I watch as the next Stuka dives on to the same place. If only I had a heavy machine gun. The aircraft is no more than 60 metres away. In a daze I lift my machine pistol and gaze along the sights. The yellow engine cover flashes past, then the face of the pilot behind the glass. Unwittingly I release two long bursts of fire.

'What are you doing, you fool?' I scold myself, waiting for the next bomb to explode. I calmed down instantly and looked around to see if anybody saw me doing something so daft, but there's no-one nearby.

After the raid, although the walls of Simon's Passage are still standing, the broken rubble and destruction can be seen through the windows. As to what's going on inside – who knows? Looking from the outside it's quiet and empty as usual. After a while, some shouting reached me.

At that moment I spot a German helmet on the other side. I fire a short burst. I listen again. Silence.

Eventually the aircraft turn their attentions elsewhere and peace returns to our section. From time to time the crack of burning buildings nearby can be heard and the rustle of shifting rubble. I settle down in my position. No Germans to be seen, nor any of our soldiers either. From time to time I can hear the rattle of a machine pistol amongst the ruins, or the long bursts of German heavy machine guns choked with the surplus of ammunition. If it wasn't for that, I could imagine I am alone.

I take stock of our situation. So, we did not succeed in breaking out. It's not obvious why or whether anyone succeeded in making it. It crosses my mind the Germans are not taking prisoners and in that case ... this is definitely it. I'm too tired to dwell on it and beyond caring anyway. I'm tormented by the lack of sleep. The mineral water I drank earlier burns unpleasantly in my stomach.

It's getting dark. Mortars and grenade launchers open fire onto our section. The rounds start falling quite close, some even into my area. Fortunately I've managed to erect a short wall of bricks, which gives me some protection from shell fragments. During a moment of silence a voice is calling me over.

I gather together my grenades arranged around me, and jump over the charred wall. It's empty, apart from a corpse lying in the doorway, but among the living a soldier I don't recognise tells me we're to retreat. He leads me to an opening in the ground above a cellar and we jump down. My guide drags me by the hand. We climb over collapsed walls, which form a sort of barricade reinforced with sandbags. I just about recognise the place from which we moved out to an attack last night. There are a few people there already. There is a murmur of voices and a clatter of weapons.

Someone, invisible in the darkness, singles me and another person out, and gives us an order more or less along the lines of 'Get the f*** behind that f****** barricade and if any f***** comes over, f****** shoot him. Retreat when you're f****** ordered.'

Then footsteps, and they move away. The other fellow goes with them. It's quiet. Empty. Only muffled explosions rolling above. The walls of the cellars give me a strong sense of security from everything flying, whistling and exploding up above. On the other hand, I am not comfortable in this unfamiliar and dark location. I try to get the feel of the barricade in front of me – a few paper sacks filled with sand. I stretch out comfortably behind them in the firing position. As usual, having the weapon in my hand calms my nerves instantly.

I struggle to stay awake. Every now and then a sound brings me to my senses and forces to focus in that direction. They're coming! No, it's an illusion. Once again I stare out into the darkness.

Hours pass, how many I don't know as I've no light to check my watch. Finally, something does happen. I'm almost certain there's someone in the cellar. Some movement and noises reach me time and again. I try to concentrate and not pay any attention to my imagination which, in this unfamiliar territory, passes towards me illusive glimmers of torchlight, or soldiers with bayonets, or a grenade flying. But this time there's definitely something there. I hear the sound of a pile of bricks being knocked over. Something crunches on the broken glass lying everywhere. Just one thought goes round my exhausted mind: I mustn't give myself away!

Now! My machine pistol judders with a short burst and the sound echoes down the long corridors. I see some flashes ahead. They're firing at me! No, it's just the sparks of my bullets hitting the walls. Immediately afterwards something moves, a few more bricks fall, followed by complete silence. One of the wounded comes up and asks me what happened. Why did I fire?

'There was someone in the cellar. Over there, by the entrance.'

'You imagined it. It was probably a rat. There are so many corpses here.'

'It wasn't a rat. Somebody tried to crawl through that hole and maybe even made it.'

'Maybe. The Germans are coming closer. Get up, we're going back to our positions.'

1 September 1944
Night time. Darkness. It's quiet and somehow empty in our old positions around the ruins of the Krasiński Palace. The wounded we were to take to the city centre, are now to go through the sewers. Obviously only those who can make it on their own can go, as we can't block the route with stretchers. I'm not sure what will happen to others. A fair number have already gone, amongst them 'Mors'

who was wounded again, and 'Gryf'. From my squad only 'Baszkir' remains. I can't see anyone I know, there are only unfamiliar faces around me. Everyone is tired, filthy and looking very glum. Nobody says anything, but somehow we all know, it's been decided we're to stay here till the end. We've all kind of expected for some time now that we'll 'get it' sooner or later, but this sudden, until now subconscious, realisation of the certainty, that it's been decided, that it will be soon, is not very pleasant. It shows on several faces that it had hit them, that they'll try to save their lives at all costs. As for me, I'm so dreadfully tired I don't feel like doing anything anymore.

Just before light we sort out our positions. We move right to the end of the ruins of the Krasiński Palace. The palace is completely gutted by fire along the whole of its length, with the exception of a small area, only partially destroyed, along Długa Street, next to the High Court buildings. The Germans have already occupied the ruins of the buildings on the side of the ghetto. For the time being we are not engaging them. Our orders are to maintain our positions in the destroyed palace. There's no possibility of retreat from here, as behind us is only the empty expanse of Krasiński Palace. The Germans are approaching the square from Bonifraterska Street, but the ruins of the High Courts, which protect the square from the direction of the ghetto, are supposedly still in our hands.

Silence reigns, interrupted only by the crackle of the burning buildings on the other side of the square, and sporadic gunfire from other sections. There was no sound of Russian artillery last night. Two girls go along the lines distributing food from a large basket. I get two whole loaves of bread and a tin of preserves. This is the last of our food stores now being distributed among the soldiers. There's no more after this. I'm not too bothered, as for the last few days I've been suffering with my stomach and am not interested in food. Apparently there's an outbreak of scarlet fever. I wonder if I've caught it.

Dawn breaks finally. Our sector is still quiet. I make myself comfortable in the rubble. Soon, the all too familiar sound of aircraft engines approaching can be heard. It's the first raid. The hall I'm in still has a remnant of a ceiling so I can't see the aircraft circling around, or where they've chosen a target. The scream of the first engine sounds uncomfortably close. The crash of falling ceilings right next to me, probably in the next room follows. I only have five seconds. I make the 15 metres to the nearest entrance to the cellars below the ruins of the palace even before deciding what to do. I jump down all the stairs leading down into the darkness in one go and fall headlong amongst the soldiers sitting and lying there.

Nothing happens. The silence is only broken by the horrible scream of the second aircraft diving. A misfire? A monstrous explosion, followed by a second and a third. The blast toppled everyone lying in the corridor. Somebody struggles on top of me, I'm lying on top of someone else. Rubble starts to fall. It's completely dark. I choke in the smoke and dust and cover my mouth and nose with the bandana I'm wearing around my neck. Somebody shouts: 'We're buried!' Someone else: 'Run!' In complete darkness I am being pushed in one direction and feel my way up the stairs. It gets a little lighter. Everybody starts running blindly towards the High Court buildings paying no attention to the crossfire in exposed places. I sit down behind a broken fragment of wall near the entrance to the cellar and try to gather my thoughts. Somebody mobilises an assembly in the ruins to count the losses. Almost half the remaining soldiers in the battalion have been lost. It turns out a bomb penetrated a cellar under the palace on the other side of the ruins from us, and buried an entire company. Someone is trying to organise a rescue party to dig out the buried. Apparently someone heard knocking and cries for help inside the collapsed cellar.

The rest of us move out to our previous positions in the rubble. Our mood improves when we see a priest in a surplice standing on a pile of rubble next to the front line, blessing each one of us as we pass.

My former position is buried, the bombs had carried away the remaining standing walls. We are now under heavy fire from the direction of the ghetto. There's lots of firing although nothing can be seen from my side. In the afternoon there is the sound of tank engines coming from somewhere very close. Their cannons and machine guns start firing from the square, somewhere behind me. The fire is so heavy that I can't retreat from my position on the side of the park. There were four of us here at the beginning, including 'Baszkir' and me. Just as the fire started from the square, one of my colleagues crawled up to me and said 'I'll go and see what's going on,' and fell to the ground, dead, as he straightened up in the narrow space behind the wall where I took shelter.

We gather our grenades together and lie still, waiting to see what happens next. A few hours pass this way.

Darkness falls prematurely, as a result of the smoke from the burning buildings. Under its cover, we crawl over towards the others. We discover that the Germans have already entered parts of the High Court buildings and are laying down fire into Krasiński Square.

We reinforce our positions to allow a greater field of fire in all directions. We can hear tanks no further than 100 metres away, but they're out of sight. A small group with a PIAT runs past and soon afterwards the explosions of the antitank weapon can be heard. It's hard to say what's going on over there, as at the same time we see silhouettes of the Germans running past. Heavy fire rains down from both sides. Hand grenades fly through the air. I fire towards the silhouettes running past, but am prevented from exposing myself by the heavy machine-gun fire which appears to be coming from three sides. I'm cut off from my friends. Things are beginning to look serious. I have only three magazines left for my machine pistol and two grenades. I decide to save ammunition and not allow myself to be taken alive. I'm sure the Germans have occupied the whole of the Old Town and are liquidating the remaining opposition. I decide it would be best to defend myself to the end from where I am.

Night falls, and the fire dies away. Voices of people moving through the rubble can be heard. I point my machine pistol in their direction but recognise familiar figures just in time. 'Baszkir' is amongst them and calls me by name. I crawl over in their direction. By the light of a rocket from the German positions I recognise 'Lot' and a few other soldiers. They say there might be a way out through the sewers if the passage has not been blocked.

We go through the rubble towards Długa Street. In the gateway of the High Court there's something resembling a parade of the remnants of the Parasol battalion. The leader is explaining how to behave once inside the sewers. We have to follow his orders precisely, only go when he orders, and to remain absolutely silent when passing under an open manhole, as the Germans are dropping grenades down them. If somebody gets seriously wounded we're to leave him in the sewers.

Our heavily wounded lie on stretchers in the rooms leading up to the gateway. They were brought here after our unsuccessful attempt to break out. Some squadrons, who have already made it out of the Old Town, managed to take their heavily wounded with them on stretchers. Now we are forbidden to take them with us. The order allows to take only the wounded that can still walk, and our weapons. The mood amongst the wounded is dreadful. Some of them pretend they can walk. It looks terrible. I go to say goodbye to my friends. All around friends and colleagues beg us to leave weapons so they can finish themselves off. I flatly refuse, but I know some of the wounded have concealed the weapons left them by others. As I'm leaving the room there's a shot at the far end. Without turning around, I run out to the gate.

I'm ordered to bring our machine gun, which was being repaired in the armoury. It's only three buildings down along Długa Street, but finding the right cellar takes me some time. The machine gun is broken, but we can't leave it. Civilians standing in gateways and cellars, seeing me thus armed, throw sullen remarks in my direction. The supportive mood of the first few days of the Uprising has gone. They only want to know if they'll be able to get into the sewers.

2 September 1944

It's getting light by the time I join up with the section. The sound of gunfire is intensifying, and there's heavy crossfire in the Krasiński Square. My friends are crouching in a long line along the wall of a ruined house on Długa Street. I can also see the opening to the sewers – a small manhole surrounded by sandbags. There's a machine gun on top of the barricade. Apart from those climbing down the manhole there's nobody here.

This area looks even more destroyed than when I last saw it. Not a single building is left standing. The barricades along Długa Street are buried under collapsed houses as to be indistinguishable. A large wheel protrudes from the huge barricade protecting the square from the direction of Miodowa Street: the last remains of the aircraft that brought us help. I note someone's managed to cut a piece of rubber out of the tyre to replace a sole of a boot. It's amazing what people will do and have time for!

The last few metres to the manhole are made under fire. I throw myself down the small opening and climb quickly down the ladder. Immediately, it is blocked by another person climbing down. There was a splash as my feet hit the bottom. I am in the sewer. First impressions: very quiet, wet feet. In fact the mud reaches to my knees. I grab the belt of the person in front of me and follow him along a low and narrow canal. To start with, we move so quickly I begin to get tired. We have to go bent double, which is not particularly comfortable. The column halts then, after a while moves off again. A halt, this time for much longer. The silence is broken by the sound of dull explosions echoing in the depths of the sewers. I'm wondering if these are the grenades that the Germans supposedly throw down the manholes.

The pauses come more frequently. At times we only move several steps. At others we cross under open drains, recognised by the increased sound of gunfire coming from above. The water there is slightly deeper and the ceiling is high enough to be able to straighten out. These moments are all too rare.

A few times I hit my head with a loud bang on some protruding pieces of wall. My friend in front of me passes me the PIAT without a word, as it's being handed down from the front of the column. For a time we carry it between us but for someone bent double it gets enormously heavy. I don't have much on me, only a pouch with a few grenades, a tin of food and my machine pistol, whose strap bites mercilessly into my neck. Were I to fall, I wouldn't have the strength to get up.

I pass the PIAT behind me. Our instructions are to take turns in carrying heavy weapons. The person following me pushes the PIAT away without saying a word. I think he doesn't understand so I explain to him in a whisper what to do. In a loud voice he replies that he won't take it, and I can stuff it up my arse.

At that moment the column moves off again so I drag the PIAT on my own, as the chap in front released his end, thinking it's been passed on. I can't move quickly carrying such a heavy weight and start to fall behind. I'm scared to lose the column, but my head is beginning to swim from fatigue. Something has to be done and quickly! I stop and try to press the PIAT into the hands of the chap following me. He replies with a stream of obscenities. I can't work out who it is. Not from our section, that's for sure. Fury rises inside me. I throw the PIAT at his feet.

'Are you taking it or not?'

He replies as before. I jerk back the bolt of my MP40 and press the barrel into his stomach. It had the desired effect. He takes the PIAT with the person behind him.

I chase after those ahead of me. There's a moment of hesitation when what sounds like the splashing of a moving column in a sewer off to one side reaches me. I decide to keep going straight on. I fall into a pool but immediately afterwards catch up with my lot.

The column stands still for a very long time. All I can think about is to be able to straighten up, if only for a minute. Behind us in the distance there's an explosion and a distinct blast. Finally the column sets off once more. The ceiling becomes much lower so that moving through the sewer becomes a torture. We pause again, but it's no rest. I've lost all sense of the time. We move on.

Suddenly, unbelievably, a light appears in the distance. We reach it. Hanging in a small niche in the ceiling is an electric light bulb! There are some telephone cables and a sign written in chalk: 'To Chmielna Street'.

We turn to one side. Shortly afterwards I feel a draft of fresh air. A drain. I climb up a ladder. Strong hands grab me under the arms and pull me out onto the surface.

I'm completely blinded. It's so light! Somebody presses a cup of coffee into my hand. Someone else offers me a cigarette. I look around. Around me all the houses are standing upright! They even have glass in the windows! People are walking around without bothering to take cover behind walls. It feels very strange.

If I close my eyes, I can still see the trails of tracer fire from Krasiński Square.

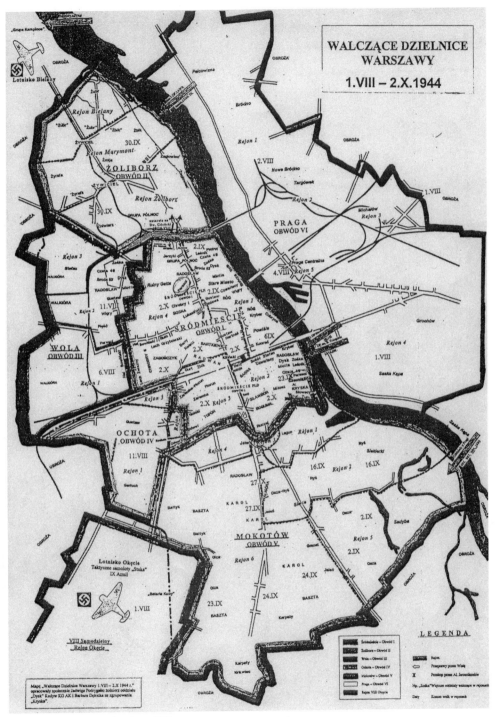

Map of the fighting districts of Warsaw.

Author's squad on a training exercise in the country prior to the Uprising.

Soldiers waiting to go into action, on the left is 'Baszkir' from author's squad.

Light armoured German vehicles on a street in Warsaw.

Ruins of Warsaw.

Ruins of Warsaw, the lower photograph is of the town square with the ruined church on the right.

Ruins of Warsaw.

A young soldier with home-made grenades.

Street urchin defenders.

Girl runner with soldiers (one wounded).

Insurgents – young and younger.

Patrol going into action.

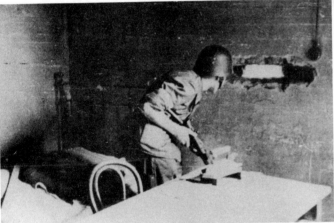

Soldier in a lookout post.

Author's sketch of a soldier at a sniper's post.

Ruins of the Old Town district.

Soldiers arriving from the Old Town to the City Centre.

Emerging from a sewer.

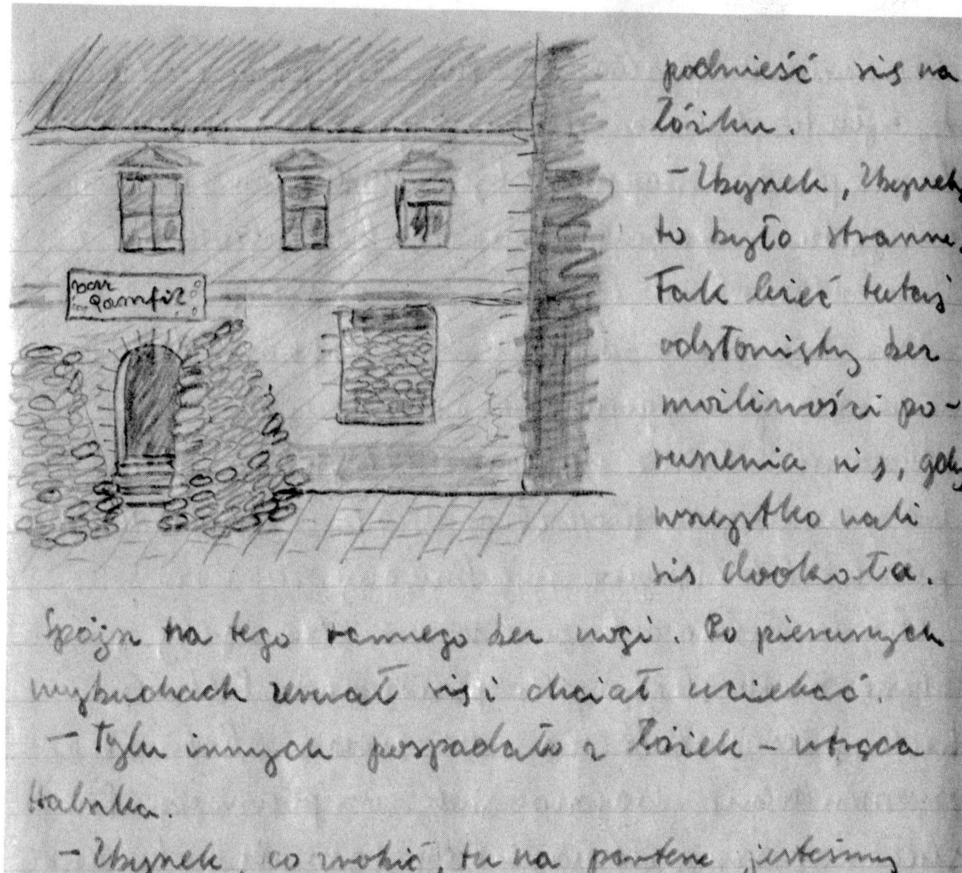

Ruins of the Warsaw Ghetto (scene of where 'Zorian' was wounded).

Ruins of Warsaw.

Warsaw burning.

Soldiers marching out of Warsaw after capitulation.

In liberated Warsaw.

The author after liberation in 1945.

The author in 1999 looking at a commemorative stone engraved with names of fallen colleagues from his squad.

PART THREE

The Aftermath

3 September 1944
Inside the Bulgarian Embassy. It's the evening. I wake up on the floor in a corridor. I don't know how long I've been asleep, maybe fifteen, maybe twenty-four hours. I can't remember clearly how I got here. Ever since I left the sewer it feels like being in another world. I remember the exit. Was it on Nowy Świat? I remember the peace and quiet, and the windows with glass still in them. Then they led us through the town. So many people! All just walking around as if there was nothing going on. Admittedly there were a few explosions but nothing very close. What do you call close? Well, close is when the smoke and dust obscures everything. What do you call really close? That's when bits of plaster land on your helmet and bricks fall around you. I must be hallucinating, because nothing like that is happening here. Even trees have leaves not blown off by explosions.

They're calling us to fall in. I get up, but my head starts spinning so badly that I have to lean against the wall. Nonetheless I go to see what's going on. If this is supposed to be the whole battalion, then it doesn't have many people. 'Lot' is here, and 'Zabawa' and a few others, but from my section only 'Baszkir'. Most people look as if they've barely washed since climbing out of the sewers, but the mood is somewhat lighter. There's talk that the sections from the Old Town will be taken to the rear to rest in some quiet sector, probably in Czerniaków, near the banks of the Vistula. It's just unbelievable. We are also thinking that when the Russians finally cross the river they will liberate us first. It's all looking very rosy. We might even survive!

In the meantime I have my own personal problems to contend with. At the moment I'm too weak to climb a set of stairs, never mind walk as far as Czerniaków, which is not very far. I go in search of our doctor. He listens to my story how I haven't eaten anything for the last few days, and even when I did, it didn't stay inside me for very long. He tells me I have scarlet fever. It appears there's an epidemic. There are no medicines in our quarters so I'm to try and get to the hospital on Śniadecka, where they'll give me some. I'll probably be able to rejoin my section the next day or the day after. I'm not very keen on parting company with my MP40. In the end I get round the situation by swapping it for a Sten. A Sten can be dismantled and hidden in a rucksack. 'Baszkir' offers to help me go to the hospital. He doesn't look brilliant himself, probably coming down with the same thing.

7 September 1944

The hospital on Śniadecka Street. It's very pleasant here. Obviously this is all relative. The pleasant thing about this place in what was once a school is that I can lie on a mattress in a corridor. It's also pleasant because we're on the second floor and not in a cellar. From time to time an explosion of a bomb or an artillery shell can be heard, but fairly far away. This morning I heard a dozen or so explosions nearby, which I immediately recognised as being the muzzle reports from a tank (it's surprising how you can become expert in these things). Apparently, from time to time tanks appear on the Mokotowski fields, to amuse themselves by shooting at the buildings overlooking the allotments. Our building is not in the first row, so there's nothing to worry about. Some locals went downstairs for shelter but I can't see the point. I listen out for machine-gun fire or grenades close by. That would indicate a German attack and then we'd have to run downstairs to help. Come to think of it, this running might be a bit of a problem, as I've only just managed to get up and can barely walk.

8 September 1944

I'm feeling much better. I can even eat and more importantly, it stays down. Having said that the food here is not what one might call varied. Every day the same 'spit soup'. It's a thick soup made with boiled grains, probably barley. It's called that because of the barley husks, which you have to spit out whilst eating it. In the Old Town there was more variety: either nothing, or plain sugar, or excellent German preserves. Curious that – why do we constantly think about food?

10 September 1944

I am practically recovered. The last dressing is to be removed from my arm tomorrow. I should mention that my arm, shot through the elbow in the first days of the uprising and almost completely healed up, has been playing me up ever since we got out of the sewers. All the various exertions and general filth didn't help.

I'm beginning to realise how lucky I am to be alive. Those last days in the Old Town weren't pleasant. That's how people probably feel when they've been sentenced to death and are awaiting execution.

I remember the ruins of the High Court buildings. The Krasiński Square coming under fire from behind. Tanks in front. No contact with anyone on either side. The German machine gun firing bursts into the wall above my head. Two magazines for my weapon, and two remaining bullets in the pocket of my jacket ... for that last moment. Then somebody pulls at my leg: 'Come on, we're going into the sewer.'

Yes. It's alright now.

11 September 1944

Great excitement last night. We heard low flying aircraft. They sounded completely different from German aeroplanes. In any case Germans don't fly at night. Why should they? They can bombard us any time they like during the day.

This means the Russians are nearby. Maybe even as far as the Vistula.

There are various rumours going around, but nobody really knows what's going on. The Russians must get here eventually, though. They can't keep waiting forever.

I'm ready to rejoin my group. Tomorrow I'll try and get to Czerniaków.

12 September 1944

I'm on my way to meet up with my group. I feel sufficiently recovered to be of some use. Czerniaków is not far away, but we're getting conflicting information. A fellow who apparently had just come from there said the Russians had landed and any moment will arrive with help. About time! On the other hand yesterday they brought a wounded casualty from Czerniaków, not from our section, but from the boys stationed next to the Parasol somewhere near Ludna Street. He spoke of heavy bombardment and a major German attack from the direction of the gas works.

This morning I climbed up to an observation post situated in one of the tallest buildings near Śniadeckie. The view from here is extensive. In our sector, the Mokotowski fields and the Polytechnic, it's quiet. There are fires burning in Mokotów, and also towards Sadyba. The largest fires are in Powiśle and probably Czerniaków. There are also explosions from what look like artillery shells.

I say goodbye to the few people I've become friendly with during my stay, and set off. In normal times, before the Uprising, it would take half an hour to walk from Śniadeckie to Czerniaków, quicker by tram. There's a thought – these days the trams are used as barricades!

To start with the going is easy until I get to Marszałkowska Street, then through some ruins and cellars to Mokotowska, finally through a ditch along Ujazdowskie Aleje towards Three Crosses Square. Here things start getting difficult. There's gunfire and explosions from the Deaf and Dumb Institute. I make my way along another ditch to the barricade next to the square. Suddenly a sound I remember well from the Old Town. Three Stukas circling over the square. Shortly afterwards I see the first one diving straight towards St Alexander's church, a large building in the centre of the square. It's only about 100 metres away. I press myself down as low as I can in the ditch. A huge explosion followed by two more. Everything gets covered with thick smoke and clouds of dust. I lie flat and check I haven't been hurt. After a while the smoke disperses. There's a huge pile of rubble where the church used to be. Not one part of the building remains standing; all three bombs must have hit their target.

I retrace my steps through the ditch and find a group of soldiers sheltering in the ruins of a building in Wiejska Street. They call out to me to take cover whilst I'm still quite a distance away, as they're coming under heavy fire. I explain I'm trying to find my way to Książęca Street and then to Czerniaków to find my section. They tell me there's no way through, but I could try and make my way around the square all the way back to Nowy Świat. Easier said than done.

I go back along the Aleje, all the way to Wilcza Street. Then through more ditches, ruins and cellars. It's almost evening by the time I get to the barricade on the corner between Nowy Świat and Książęca. Here I find more people trying to get to Czerniaków. There's one soldier in a battle dress similar to mine. He's from the

Zośka battalion, just making his way back from his mother's funeral, who died in a building near Złota Street. He tells me the Parasol battalion is stationed right next to them. He knows 'Luty' and a few others from my company.

The route to Czerniaków goes through a long and a fairly deep ditch dug right down the middle of Książęca Street. There's heavy fire from grenade launchers. As it gets dark, we can see tracer fire from machine guns flying just above the ditch. We would like to know what's going on in Czerniaków, but somehow no-one's coming from the opposite direction. People are starting to run the few steps from where we're standing, and dive into the ditch. Soon it's my turn. Darkness all around and smoke coming from a nearby burning building (possibly St Lazarus' hospital). Shells and grenades exploding nearby. I see someone on the other side helping a casualty. I recognise my friend from the Zośka battalion. I reach a place where some of our soldiers are blocking the way. They're standing or lying with their weapons aimed along the ditch.

'Germans ahead. No way through.'

13 September 1944

I'm back in Śniadeckie. I spent the whole of last night and some of today in a cellar next to Książęca Street waiting for an opportunity to get through. Instead, the bombardment and gunfire grew heavier. There's no way of reaching my section. I'm ashamed to admit that in the end hunger forced me back to where I started from yesterday. When I was still in hospital, and was just about able to walk, I became friendly with some of the lads occupying the sector opposite the polytechnic. I decide to join them. I present myself to the Major in charge of the section. He takes me on gladly, probably not so much for my personal attributes as for my Sten gun, which I've managed to hold onto.

15 September 1944

Still in Śniadeckie. It's like being on God's hearthrug here, as the saying goes. Obviously, this feeling of comfort is relative. There's a fine barricade across the street protecting the square in front of the polytechnic from the occupied parts of Warsaw. Further to one side are open fields, the allotments on Mokotowskie. The Germans are dug in, several hundred metres from our positions on the other side of the fields. They are clearly upset that the buildings along Polna Street, although partially damaged, look over their positions in the fields. From time to time, a few tanks arrive and fire a few shots into the buildings. Then peace returns, that is, if you don't count the snipers and bursts of machine-gun fire aimed at the windows. We don't fire back as there's not much ammunition, and what we have we must save in case of a frontal attack.

18 September 1944
All I can think about is food. Ever since I recovered I could eat all day. The food situation is not good; there's a steady supply of barley soup from the kitchen but, as they say, there's too much of it to die of hunger, but not enough to live on.

Yesterday I had a marvellous stroke of luck. One of our various duties is keeping watch in the observation posts on the roofs or upper storeys of the houses overlooking the Mokotowskie fields. You sit there for hours with binoculars and observe. Obviously it's important not to be observed yourself. The Germans don't know exactly where we are, and every now and then spray the buildings with machine-gun fire here and there. Sometimes they find a real target. And so, yesterday, as I was looking out over the foreground trying to find their positions, one of them must have spotted me. A long burst of fire crashed into my window. Fortunately it was a fraction high; otherwise I wouldn't be writing this. They quickly corrected themselves and the bullets crashed into the bricks and other pieces of rubble I had filled the window frame with. Needless to say, by this time I was in the next room flat on the floor.

After this little mishap we decide to move to another floor. The building was damaged some time ago from an artillery shell, or by a tank down in the fields. Scrambling around through the rubble we discovered a door to a kitchen cupboard or a pantry. Searching around we found a huge paper sack filled with crusts of bread, about 20 kilograms in all. It must have been there some time, as the bread was stone hard. Not that this is a problem, as we all have good teeth. The worst part was that each crust was riddled with a network of little tunnels made by tiny maggots. When we carried our booty back to the quarters our colleagues take differing views. Some say they won't ever eat anything so revolting, others quite the opposite, that it doesn't bother them at all and that maggots are as good as butter or dripping. My opinion is somewhere between the two: I bite off a small piece and tap the crust against something hard until the maggots fall out. I bite off another piece, and carry on. It's a slow but it's a perfectly pleasant way of spending long hours on guard when nothing happens.

22 September 1944
Today I ate my fill for the first time in ages. It happened like this. From our observation post overlooking the Mokotowskie fields, we could see on some nights a certain commotion down below. The German machine guns suddenly start firing very low over the fields. From time to time they fire white flares, which illuminate everything as if at daylight. The Mokotowskie fields are covered in allotments all the way from our positions near Polna Street, right up to the German lines. On very dark nights groups of civilians crawl out into the fields looking for things to eat – vegetables, tomatoes, potatoes. Unfortunately, German patrols also move around from time to time. This situation has lasted right from the start of the Uprising. It is probably the only front line in the whole of Warsaw that hasn't changed since that time. I fall in with a group of civilians, all young men, typical Warsaw artful dodgers. They make me an offer which I could not refuse. They need someone with a weapon to protect them. In return they'll share their spoils with me.

And so last night, I wasn't on duty and it was very dark. I went out first, across the street and into the allotments. You have to crawl out very low, flat on your stomach. The vegetation here is of variable heights as it has been thoroughly raided, sometimes a few centimetres, sometimes almost a metre high. Potatoes, carrots, nettles, all sorts. I crawl along right up to the German positions. My job is to keep watch and, if a German patrol should appear, to open fire, giving the people a chance to escape. I'm quite close to the German trenches; at times I can hear German voices. Worse still, I can also distinctly hear the sound of digging behind me and even voices speaking in Polish. I wanted to shout 'keep quiet' but obviously can't. I lie in some furrow keeping as flat as I can, aware there's a machine-gun nest not very far away. A rocket goes up for me to observe just how close it is. I think I've crawled too far. I lie still, too scared to move and give away my position.

An hour or two pass in this fashion. Nothing happens but behind me, in the fields, quite a commotion is going on. I'm sure more people joined our group. After a time it must have dawned on the Germans there's something going on. The machine gun wakes up, and opens fire just above the ground. Tracer fire whips over my head. The commotion behind me dies down. The Germans quickly got bored and settled down again.

As it starts to get light, I crawl carefully back to our positions. I must admit my partners have given me a very fair share. I get a small sack of potatoes and two tomatoes. I eat the tomatoes straight away but what am I supposed to do with raw potatoes? During the day I set off towards Marszałkowska Street to do some 'trading'. Another stroke of luck. I meet a friendly family whose house is not completely destroyed. They can still cook and have some supplies. They accept my potatoes gladly and in return give me quite a decent meal, barley with potatoes and something else. I must keep up their acquaintance.

24 September 1944

Morning. I've been on the observation post on the top storey of a house on Polna Street since midnight. It's getting light, it's going to be a nice day, and there's some good news. There have been more Russian aeroplanes overnight. I'm intrigued by their pilots' tactics. The aircraft approaches just above the roofs with its engine turned off, or on very low revolutions, completely silent and totally invisible in the darkness. Then a sudden growl from the engine and if at that particular moment you look in the right direction, you can just about see a shadow of an aeroplane. Then the engine cuts out, and it disappears again. Sometimes there's a burst of tracer fire from the German positions on the other side of the fields in the direction where the aircraft was. These games last all night.

Now the sun rises, and the stage, in this case the skies above Warsaw, is taken over by the Germans. I can hear the rumble of large aircraft. I spot them soon afterwards, flying in our direction. I start to feel uncomfortable. Up until this time I had never seen more than three or four German aircraft in one formation. I count them ... five ... ten ... twenty-seven! If all this is intended for us here, it's the end. I know fully well how much damage only three aircraft can do.

I can now see where they're heading for: Mokotów. I've been in that observation post many times, and I know the terrain of our foreground pretty well. From here we have the best view over the Mokotowskie fields, Okęcie and Mokotów. A little further away are the districts of Sadyba and the outer Mokotów. The taller blocks of flats and small villas shining in the sunlight are clearly outlined. Everything is out in the open, completely undefended. There might have been some anti-aircraft fire from the other side of the Vistula, but can't be seen from here. But what can be seen quite clearly through the binoculars are the bombs breaking away from the planes. Huge pillars of fire and rubble rise into the air and smoke obscures everything. The whole of Mokotów is now covered with a thick cloud of smoke, through which the aircraft dive repeatedly. There is also artillery fire and bursts of machine-gun fire in the distance. No doubt about it, the attack on Mokotów has started. I send a messenger off to the headquarters with the news.

My morale plummets. The euphoria I felt after escaping from the Old Town has gone. What now? I got out of there alive, but it seems like a stay of sentence rather than a reprieve. Here it may be like being on a God's hearthrug, but for how much longer? From my observation post I can see the situation developing as if on a stage. The Germans surround one neighbourhood after another and obliterate it. We can't help the people there, nor they us. Since I've been here districts have fallen one by one: Powiśle, Sadyba, Czerniaków, and now Mokotów. It's obvious our turn will come in the next few days. How long will it all last? It doesn't make much difference, maybe a few days, maybe a week. The houses here are still standing and are relatively solid, but we have far fewer weapons and provisions than in the Old Town. And also there is the fact the Germans are not taking prisoners. Obviously every soldier is prepared for the possibility that he might die, but there's a big difference between 'might' and 'must'. Too much thinking! It's just as well we're being relieved and can go to lunch.

1 October 1944

Today something most unusual happened. Silence reigned in my section of the barricade on 6th August Street. Not even gunfire. Suddenly, a group of people appeared through the passage on our side, among them officers I've never seen before. They gave me an order: to make a way through the barricade. A delegation will be passing through. What? Where? Where are they going? What's going on?

It appears I'm the least well-informed person in the whole of Warsaw. It seems there's a possibility we can surrender, and the Germans will take us prisoner and not execute us as they have been doing so far. Apparently the British and the Americans have officially recognised the Home Army (*Armia Krajowa*) fighting in Warsaw as part of the normal fighting forces protected by the Geneva Convention. So there's a possibility we might get out alive. In any case there's new hope, the same feeling as when I heard there was a way out through the sewers in the Old Town. Afterwards that hope began to crumble, when the districts of Warsaw fell one by one.

But, can the Germans be trusted? Might they not pretend to take us prisoner only to wipe us out in some concentration camp?

2 October 1944

The palace in front of the polytechnic is quiet and empty. I've spent a long time observing this area from a distance from our observation posts in the houses along Śniadeckie and 6th August Street. The main entrance to the polytechnic is to the right. Ahead of us, the hospital buildings occupied by the Germans. To the left, just before the Mokotowskie fields a small chapel where candles were lit before the Uprising. It's a flat paved area. On our side is the barricade and reinforced houses. The silence is deceptive. There are machine-gun nests on the side of the polytechnic and the hospital, holding the square in a crossfire. To step out into this area means certain death.

But right now it's quiet. A ceasefire. You can stand on the barricade and nobody opens up. Indeed, what is happening is very strange. From the German side a group of officers emerge holding a white flag. From our side too, a group of people, also with a white sheet on a stick: several officers and some civilians. They walk across the square towards the German group and disappear around the corner.

3 October 1944

The surrender has been signed for certain. We now have all the details. We have been officially recognised as allied soldiers. We are allowed to leave Warsaw with our weapons and standards. It's unbelievable. I wonder where we'll find the standards? Also I don't see how it'll work with the weapons either. According to the pact we'll surrender only to the Wehrmacht. The SS, the Gestapo, the military police and similar, will not be involved. We will be treated as prisoners of war, under the Geneva Convention.

There's a strange atmosphere in my sector. To start with, they've handed out all the remaining provisions, so suddenly we have plenty to eat. They also divided up the treasury. Somebody handed me 1,500 złoty. There is also talk we might be getting dollars. Maybe somebody else did get some, but I personally never received any. We were supposed to get them later, but obviously later never came. It doesn't matter in any case. It's difficult to decide what to do with the weapons. We're supposed to walk out carrying them, and hand them to the Germans. I've become quite attached to my weapon during all these days. Parting with my Sten gun is unimaginable. I always thought we'd be together till the end. Mind you, the end was supposed to be different.

We talk about it amongst ourselves. If the agreement with the Germans is that we're to walk out carrying weapons, then we should keep to our side of it. If we leave without weapons they might think we've hidden them, and could start making us tell them where. Some say the exact opposite, that if the Germans see anyone with a weapon they'll shoot them on the spot without further ado.

In the end we decide as follows: I buried my Sten and the magazines in the cellar of one of the houses along Śniadeckie Street. One of my colleagues gave me an ancient pre-war Polish rifle without a bolt to carry instead.

We also have to provision ourselves for the march to captivity. I fasten a small potato sack to my splendid leather webbing, which previously carried magazines and ammunition pouches for my Sten gun, and on occasions, the hand grenades – and here it is – I've a knapsack. A blanket or something to cover myself with would come in handy, as we might be held captive until the winter. This is difficult, as others more enterprising than I have made off with everything already.

I had more luck with the rest of my equipment. I manage to get hold of a warm jumper. A civilian sold me a fairly decent overcoat for my 1,500 złoty. Apart from that I have my big silver spoon from which I won't part. A soldier never knows when they might be serving soup.

4 October 1944

Ożarów. So, it turned out to be true after all. We've left Warsaw and we're now prisoners of war. I have very mixed feelings. On the one hand the Uprising failed, on the other hand I am alive. We knew the Uprising would fail even before the Old Town fell. Our hopes were raised in the Town Centre when there were rumours of landings or help from the other side of the Vistula (where the Russian front was stationed), but for the last week it started to look as if they would finish us off after all. This time we couldn't have relied even on a handy sewer. Where could we have gone? We were in the last district left standing.

In the final days, I've witnessed important events. The people negotiating the truce went through our barricade. We dismantled the same barricade to facilitate the march out from our sector.

It was quite an occasion. Our section marched out second. From our position on the barricade waiting for our turn, I had a good view of those who came out first. They fell in along 6th August Street and marched past us. I didn't recognise any of them. Apparently it was some infantry brigade. I never knew we had brigades but, I imagine, now that we are a 'real' army, we need to have brigades. Either way, they were marching very smartly. Four columns, an officer in front, followed by the soldiers. The first four carried weapons. They also carried standards, probably the Polish flags that were hanging from houses at the start of the Uprising. It all looked very impressive. They passed the barricade and marched in a long column across the empty square towards the polytechnic. The Germans were on the other side next to their positions in the hospital.

It was our turn next. We formed up in fours. Those with weapons were at the front. We had flags, but I daren't think how it all looked. Those of us in front still had some sort of uniforms: Polish, German, railwaymen's and others. In the column were also our girls – colleagues, messengers, nurses. Finally a few of the youngest, the underground messengers and others, those thirteen to fourteen year olds. But everyone had a white and red band tied around their arm. I was in the second row from the front on the side and could clearly see the goings on. Eventually the order came.

'Quick march!'

We set off. A little irregularly to start with. It's just as well we were a good few metres from the barricade, it gave us time to fall into step. Left ... left ... left right left.

It wasn't too bad considering we'd never been on parade together before. We got to our partially dismantled barricade. There was a group of officers and civilians standing there. They all looked important. Maybe Bór-Komorowski (commander of the AK Polish Underground Movement) himself was there? I had no idea what he looked like. The officer in front saluted. We replied with a sort of 'eyes right'. Now we were marching across the empty square. Tension mounted. The Germans are close. We are now in their territory, in their positions between the hospital and the Polytechnic. They were firing at us from here. We were now able to see their positions from close up. Quite a large group of officers and soldiers were carrying machine pistols ready to fire. They were probably worried in case we threw ourselves on them. I hadn't been this close to a German for a long time. But the only shots they took were from cameras. All the more reason to look as military as possible.

We kept marching down Nowowiejska Street along the side of the polytechnic and into Filtrowa Street. The road was empty, but every 10 metres on either side stood soldiers with a gun. They were indeed the Wehrmacht, most of them quite elderly. A few of them even had tears in their eyes. I imagine they were most moved by the sight of the youngest boys – the messengers – and the girls in uniform with red and white armbands.

We marched all the way to Narutowicza Square. The buildings on either side were still standing, although you could see the marks of the battles on them. We went through a wide gateway into what looked like a school. Here the atmosphere got less pleasant. The whole courtyard was surrounded by machine-gun nests, with gunners ready to fire. Was this a trick? They could easily polish us off here. But no. In the centre of the courtyard was a big pile of weapons. Rifles, Sten guns, Russians antitank weapons, and others. We approached one by one or in pairs, and threw our weapons onto the pile. After that we were individually searched, not very thoroughly, and pushed through another exit. They didn't even take my watch, possibly because I fastened it above my elbow.

They made us fall into another column. After a while we started to march out to the west, away from Warsaw. We reached our destination in the evening. Now we're in a factory of The Ożarów Cable Company surrounded by soldiers. We entered the empty factory buildings. All the machines and equipment have been taken away. We stretch ourselves out as best we can on the concrete floors. It's cold and dark.

8 October 1944
A wagon train to Berlin. It's pleasant, relatively speaking. I'm one of fifty-seven passengers stuffed into a smallish wagon. The wagon itself is locked and bolted. There's a small window high up firmly boarded over. It's packed tight. There's not enough room to lie down, I can only sit hunched up against the wall. I have my own window however, and only share it with one of my colleagues. It should be mentioned that this window is a hole about 4 centimetres in diameter, carved out of the wooden sides of the wagon with a penknife. There are around twenty similar 'windows' in our wagon. The first one was cut out during the night when the train was moving. We were worried what the Germans might do when they saw it in daylight. The train moved very slowly and stopped several times but nothing happened. The Germans are sticking to the agreement and we're indeed guarded by the Wehrmacht, and not by the SS or the Vlassov men. This Wehrmacht is in fact Volkssturm, comprised of the last conscription of elderly people. Even if they're not exactly friendly towards us, they are certainly not unfriendly. I found out from those who have spoken to them that they just do what they're told, waiting for the war to end.

During one of our halts I volunteer to bring water. We stop at a small station, there are some wagons around and some rubble. I go with a guard along our train. Each wagon has as many perforations as a sieve. It appears they didn't find any penknives when we were searched!

The train finally got moving after a few hours and several more stops. Right now we've halted for good and have been standing for several hours. We must be either in Berlin or very close. The train is standing on an embankment from which we have a good view on either side. During the night we could see fires burning on the horizon on both sides.

Then a heavy artillery barrage can be heard. At least one gun emplacement is not far away from the tracks. It's an air raid! It's rather unpleasant as we are stuck in this train on the embankment exposed from all sides. Obviously it's impossible to escape from closed wagons. Train tracks are frequent targets for air raids. The bombs start to fall. They fall far away to start with, then closer. The nearest explosion was no more than a few hundred metres away from us. I've never experienced anything like it. Successive explosions blend into one continuous noise. I can distinctly feel the ground swaying underneath me. It must be one of those famous air raids with a thousand bombers that we heard about on the BBC.

Serves them right. That's for Warsaw!

Epilogue

This collection of memories cannot be the complete history of a group of ten boys, which at one time was the first squad, second platoon, third company of the Scouting Battalion Parasol (the Umbrella). We got together in occupied Warsaw mainly through the underground school called the Lelewel. After that came the underground scouting movement, the trips outside Warsaw, the scout camps where we used to sing old scouting songs. Who would have thought that a few years later they'd be singing songs about us?

Seven of us died there: in Wola, Starówka (the Old Town) and Czerniaków. In many cases the exact circumstances of the death aren't clear as the witnesses also died. Some bodies were never found or were not identified. Their only mark are their pseudonyms engraved on the Parasol monument in the Warsaw military cemetery of Powązki.

Of the three who survived ...
'Baszkir' was the only one in our squad who wasn't wounded. We were together for a while in the prisoner of war camp at Stalag XB in Sandbostel, near Bremen. After the liberation he stayed for a while in Germany then returned to Poland to his family. Due to his young age (he was sixteen during the Uprising) he wasn't arrested by the UB (Polish communist secret police) after the war. He studied engineering and lives in Warsaw.

'Sławek' was heavily wounded in Czerniaków, one of the few who escaped the slaughter of the wounded. He was bundled into a boat and transported to the right bank of the Vistula, and spent many months in hospitals. He was the eldest amongst us (during the Uprising he was twenty years old), and unfortunately could not escape the notice of the UB, who made his life difficult after the war. Despite this he finished his studies and lives in Warsaw.

'Deivir', the author. After the liberation from prisoner of war camps in Germany the main topic of conversation was: what next? Nobody was under any illusions we will be welcomed back home as 'the heroes who fought for freedom'. There was plenty of time in the prisoner of war camps to realise that those who were about to 'liberate' our country would not be well disposed towards 'reactionaries' like us. Several newspapers reached the POW camps from Poland, filled with vitriolic rhetoric against the principles which we considered normal and had fought for. Then we started to hear stories about people from Parasol and their families being arrested and interrogated. Those who were involved with the assassination of Kutschera (Head of the Warsaw Police District) were considered particularly dangerous. All this news was not encouraging to return home.

As for me, I always dreamt about being an engineer, to make new machines and installations. These opportunities were available in England. That's where I ended up after a journey across the Alps to the Polish division stationed in Italy, from there to transit camps in England and, finally, a university in London.

Zbigniew George Czajkowski
February 1999

Index

Stackpole Military History Series

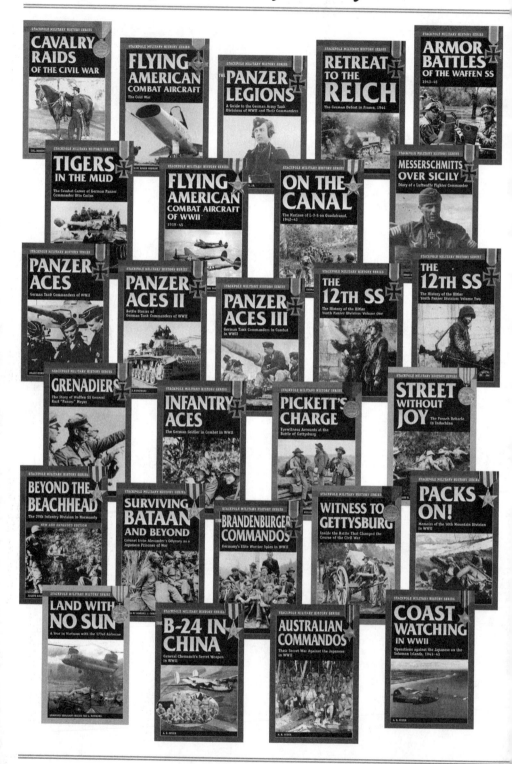

Real battles. Real soldiers. Real stories.

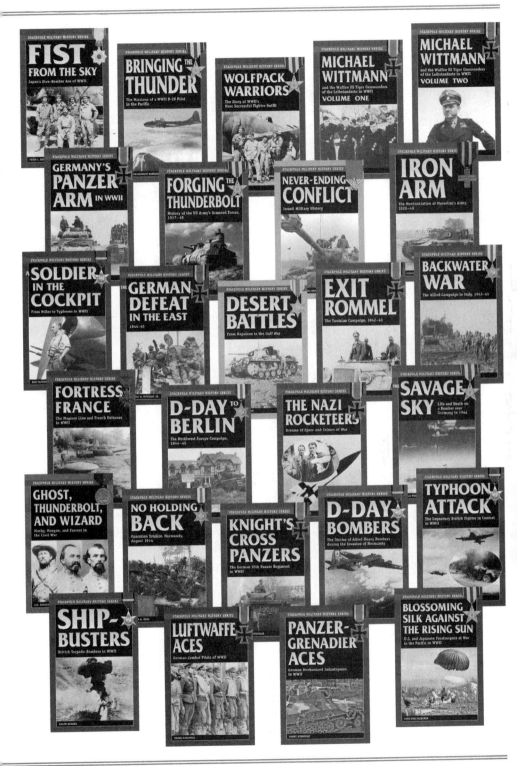

Stackpole Military History Series

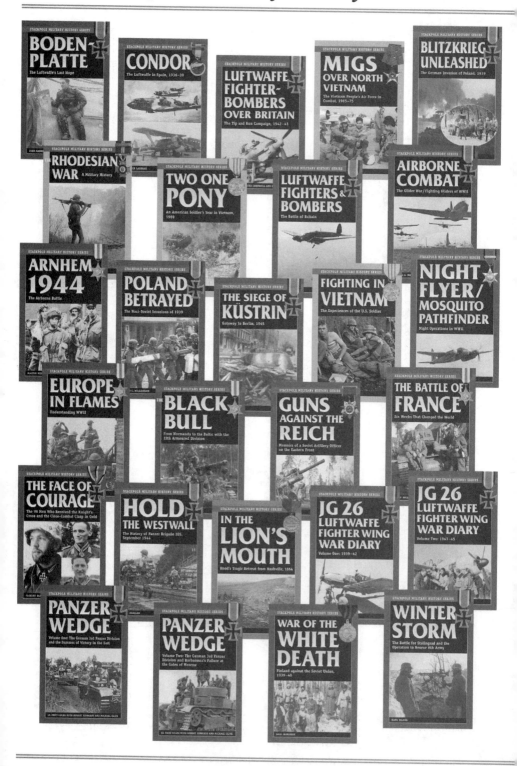

Real battles. Real soldiers. Real stories.

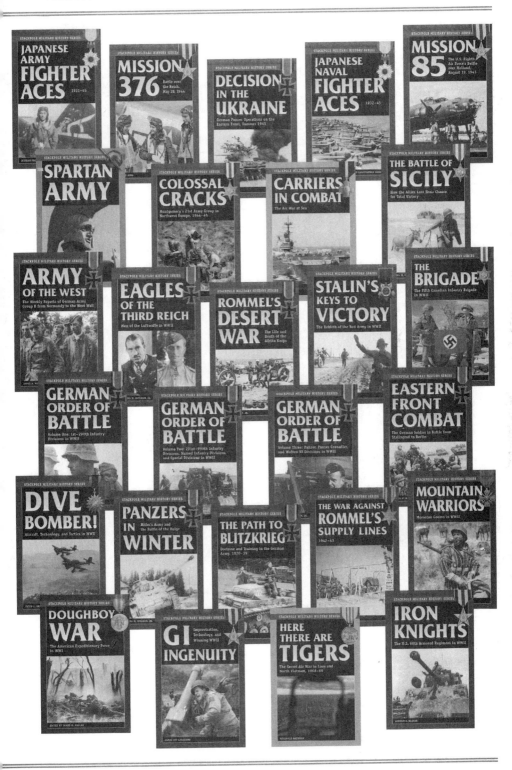

Stackpole Military History Series

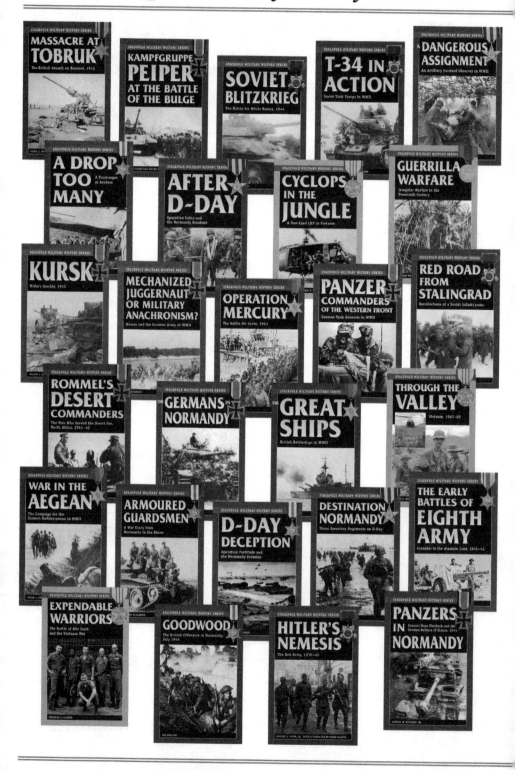

Real battles. Real soldiers. Real stories.

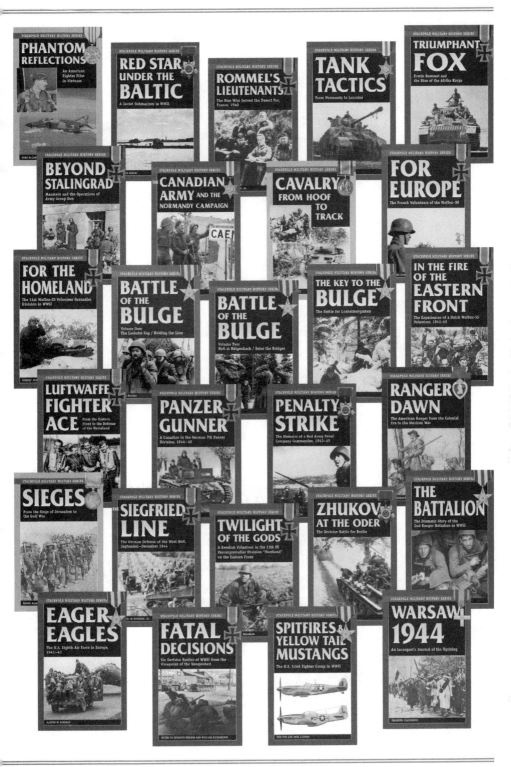

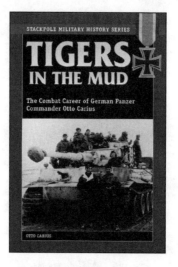

Stackpole Military History Series

ARMOR BATTLES
OF THE WAFFEN-SS
1943–45
Will Fey, translated by Henri Henschler

The Waffen-SS were considered the elite of the
German armed forces in the Second World War and
were involved in almost continuous combat. From
the sweeping tank battle of Kursk on the Russian
front to the bitter fighting among the hedgerows
of Normandy and the offensive in the Ardennes,
these men and their tanks made history.

Paperback • 6 x 9 • 384 pages • 32 photos, 15 drawings, 4 maps

WWW.STACKPOLEBOOKS.COM
1-800-732-3669

Stackpole Military History Series

GRENADIERS
THE STORY OF WAFFEN SS GENERAL
KURT "PANZER" MEYER
Kurt Meyer

Known for his bold and aggressive leadership, Kurt
Meyer was one of the most highly decorated German
soldiers of World War II. As commander of various
units, from a motorcycle company to the Hitler Youth
Panzer Division, he saw intense combat across Europe,
from the invasion of Poland in 1939 to the 1944
campaign for Normandy, where he fell into Allied
hands and was charged with war crimes.

Paperback • 6 x 9 • 448 pages • 93 b/w photos

Stackpole Military History Series

KURSK
HITLER'S GAMBLE
Walter S. Dunn, Jr.

During the summer of 1943, Germany unleashed its last major offensive on the Eastern Front and sparked the epic battle of Kursk, which included the largest tank engagement in history. Marked by fiery clashes between German Tigers and Soviet T-34s in the mud and dust of western Russia, the campaign began well enough for the Germans, but the Soviets counterattacked and eventually forced Hitler to end the operation. When it was over, thousands lay dead or wounded on both sides, but the victorious Red Army had turned the tide of World War II in the East.

Paperback • 6 x 9 • 240 pages • 9 photos, 1 map

Stackpole Military History Series

T-34 IN ACTION
SOVIET TANK TROOPS IN WORLD WAR II
Artem Drabkin and Oleg Sheremet

Regarded by many as the best tank of World War II, the Soviet T-34 was fast, well-armored, and heavily gunned—more than a match for the German panzers. From Moscow to Kiev, Leningrad to Stalingrad, Kursk to Berlin, T-34s rumbled through the dust, mud, and snow of the Eastern Front and propelled the Red Army to victory. These firsthand accounts from Soviet tankmen evoke the harrowing conditions they faced: the dirt and grime of battlefield life, the claustrophobia inside a tank, the thick smoke and deafening blasts of combat, and the bloody aftermath.

Paperback • 6 x 9 • 208 pages • 40 photos, 5 maps

Stackpole Military History Series

BEYOND THE BEACHHEAD
THE 29TH INFANTRY DIVISION IN NORMANDY
Joseph Balkoski

Previously untested in battle, the American 29th
Infantry Division stormed Omaha Beach on D-Day and
began a summer of bloody combat in the hedgerows
of Normandy. Against a tenacious German foe, the
division fought fiercely for every inch of ground and,
at great cost, liberated the town of St. Lô. This new
and expanded edition of Joseph Balkoski's classic
follows the 29th through the final stages of the
campaign and the brutal struggle for the town of Vire.

Paperback • 6 x 9 • 352 pages • 36 b/w photos, 30 maps

WWW.STACKPOLEBOOKS.COM
1-800-732-3669

Stackpole Military History Series

BRINGING THE THUNDER
THE MISSIONS OF A WWII B-29 PILOT IN THE PACIFIC
Gordon Bennett Robertson, Jr.

By March 1945, when Ben Robertson took to the skies above
Japan in his B-29 Superfortress, the end of World War II in the
Pacific seemed imminent. But although American forces were
closing in on its home islands, Japan refused to surrender, and
American B-29s were tasked with hammering Japan to its
knees with devastating bomb runs. That meant flying low-
altitude, nighttime incendiary raids under threat of flak,
enemy fighters, mechanical malfunction, and fatigue. It may
have been the beginning of the end, but just how soon the
end would come—and whether Robertson and his crew would
make it home—was far from certain.

Paperback • 6 x 9 • 304 pages • 36 b/w photos, 1 map

WWW.STACKPOLEBOOKS.COM
1-800-732-3669

Stackpole Military History Series

FLYING AMERICAN COMBAT AIRCRAFT OF WWII

1939–45

Robin Higham, editor

From bombing raids in the flak-filled skies over
Germany and Japan to cargo runs above the snowy
Himalayas and wheeling dogfights in nimble fighters,
American aircraft contributed to victory in all theaters
of World War II. Written by the former aviators
themselves, these riveting accounts take the reader
into the cockpits of such storied and beloved
warplanes as the B-17 Flying Fortress, the P-40
Kittyhawk, the P-51 Mustang, and many more.

Paperback • 6 x 9 • 368 pages • 73 b/w photos

WWW.STACKPOLEBOOKS.COM
1-800-732-3669

Stackpole Military History Series

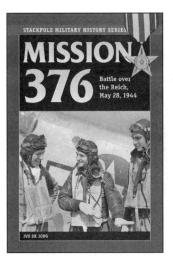

MISSION 376
BATTLE OVER THE REICH, MAY 28, 1944
Ivo de Jong

Some of the U.S. Eighth Air Force's bombing missions of World War II, such as the raid on the ball-bearing factories at Schweinfurt, became legendary. Many others did not, but these more routine missions formed an important part of Allied strategy. One of them was Mission 376 on May 28, 1944, when more than 1,200 American B-17s and B-24s took off from bases in England and headed for targets inside Germany, where Luftwaffe fighters scrambled to beat them back. With unprecedented and enthralling detail, this book describes an "ordinary" bombing mission during World War II.

Paperback • 6 x 9 • 448 pages • 329 b/w photos

WWW.STACKPOLEBOOKS.COM
1-800-732-3669

Stackpole Military History Series

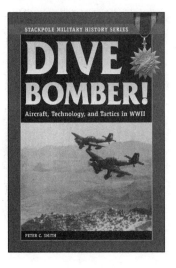

DIVE BOMBER!
AIRCRAFT, TECHNOLOGY, AND TACTICS IN WWII
Peter C. Smith

It is a dive bomber that provides one of the most dramatic images of World War II: a German Stuka screaming toward the ground as part of the blitzkrieg that opened the war. Almost all the major combatants developed dive bombers, from the Japanese Val to the American Dauntless and Soviet Pe-2. In this illustrated history of Allied and Axis dive bombers, military historian Peter C. Smith traces these formidable aircraft from the earliest test runs to their emergence as devastatingly effective weapons in the Pacific and Mediterranean, on the Eastern Front, and in Western Europe.

Paperback • 6 x 9 • 400 pages • 69 photos, 26 diagrams

WWW.STACKPOLEBOOKS.COM
1-800-732-3669

Stackpole Military History Series

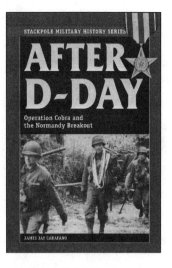

AFTER D-DAY
OPERATION COBRA AND THE NORMANDY BREAKOUT
James Jay Carafano

After storming the beaches on D-Day, June 6, 1944, the Allied invasion of France bogged down in seven weeks of grueling attrition in Normandy. On July 25, U.S. divisions under Gen. Omar Bradley launched Operation Cobra, an attempt to break out of the hedgerows and begin a war of movement against the Germans. Despite a disastrous start, with misdropped bombs killing more than 100 GIs, Cobra proved to be one of the most pivotal battles of World War II, successfully breaking the stalemate in Normandy and clearing a path into the heart of France.

Paperback • 6 x 9 • 336 pages • 31 b/w photos, 10 maps